# *Endorsements*

Thought-provoking, challenging, powerful, a unique look at eternal truth—these were a few of my thoughts after reading *Becoming His*. Author Jenny Erlingsson reminded me to rethink and ponder old truths in a new and wonderful way. Those truths are: an infinite, eternal God, a world of circumstances, an endless diversity of personalities…divinely brought together to manifest His Glory! Men, do not back away from reading this book. Its truth is truly universal. This is one of the best I've read. Get ready; I believe one of the greatest Christian authors of our time has just been launched!

—Curtis S Silcox
Evangelist and Founder
Good News Today and SEASON

I have been gripped with a strong sense of the Lord's release on His daughters in this season. There is no doubt in my mind that we are about to see a new wind of holy liberation hit women of God, true Christ-followers all over this globe. The spirit of religion tells women to be quiet in church, yet the Spirit of God is saying that it's time for the lionesses of God to roar (Joel 2:28). I'm convinced that a third Great Awakening is incumbent…but it won't get off the ground, if half the army of the Lord is on mute. So Heaven is raising up fresh voices to call this movement out.

Jenny Erlingsson is such a voice, and a timely one at that. I have known Jenny for a number of years, and I have seen her faithfully serve the Body of Christ and be actively involved in women's ministries and discipleship. She has a heart for equipping and building up women like few people that I know. I am SO excited for this book that you hold in your hands and believe that it will challenge you to go deeper in what God has for you and call out gifting that has been placed in you for such a time as this. So get ready to be transformed and released to your next level.

—SEAN SMITH
Director of Sean Smith Ministries/Pointblank Intl.
Author of *I Am Your Sign* and *Prophetic Evangelism*
@revseansmith
www.seansmithministries.com

*Becoming His* is a powerful tool that women will read, relate to, and see glimpses of who they are in almost every biblical character. Jenny brings reality and authenticity throughout her book as she unwraps each woman's strength and weakness and helps the reader to apply life lessons in their own journey of understanding the power of their story!

—PASTOR LAURA LEE,
Church Alive Assembly of God
Fuquay-Varina, NC

# Becoming HIS

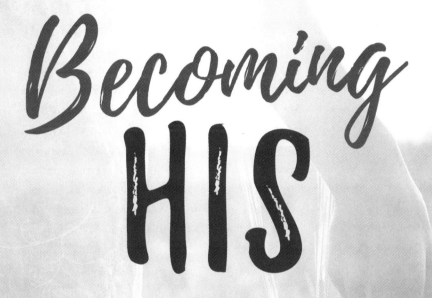

## FINDING YOUR PLACE AS A
### *Daughter of God*

JENNY ERLINGSSON

DESTINY IMAGE® PUBLISHERS, INC.

P.O. Box 310, Shippensburg, PA 17257-0310

"Promoting Inspired Lives."

This book and all other Destiny Image and Destiny Image Fiction books are available at Christian bookstores and distributors worldwide.

Cover design by Prodigy Pixel

Interior design by Terry Clifton

For more information on foreign distributors, call 717-532-3040.

Reach us on the Internet: www.destinyimage.com.

ISBN 13 TP: 978-0-7684-1072-3

ISBN 13 eBook: 978-0-7684-1073-0

For Worldwide Distribution, Printed in the U.S.A.

1 2 3 4 5 6 7 8 / 20 19 18 17 16

# Dedication

This book is dedicated to my husband Bjarni and children Nyema, Thor and Eyja. I never knew how much marriage was a mirror. I never knew how much children revealed the Father. Thank you for teaching me how to be HIS.

# Acknowledgments

Although long-hoped for, I don't know if I ever really believed I would be here. The scribbles and stories I penned as a 3-year-old have long been swept away with time, but the desire and passion to write have never wavered. And here I am…writing down a list of those that I want to thank the most within the pages of a book that you will soon immerse yourself in. What a wonder life is. Dreams can sometimes feel like the faintest of things, wispy tendrils of our imagination and longings that sometimes don't come to fruition in our own lifetimes. So when we have the opportunity to see one come to life, it is truly a wonder to behold. A beautiful thing. And even more beautiful are the ones who walk the journey out with us. I will do the cliché thing and say that if I were to thank everyone that I want to and need to I could fill this entire book with just their praises. So friends, know that there is an entire book dedicated to you in my heart even if these pages don't visibly show all of your names. There are some that were vital in the creation process of this book that I have the privilege to call out, so to speak, and honor.

My plan was to self-publish this work, but after looking through a few of the books that I own, I decided to read more about Destiny Image. I immediately fell in love with their vision and decided to take a chance and submit my manuscript to them. I am so thankful for the entire team at Destiny Image. The books that you publish are changing the world one life at a time, and it is such an honor to be a part. Special thanks go to Sierra White, my acquisitions agent and project manager. You believed in and loved this book from the start. Every email and communication from you were constant reminders of the reality of my dream and for that I am grateful. Thanks also to Tammy Fitzgerald, my editor, and Terry Clifton for the beautiful book design. Your work and creativity turned my words into art and substance.

For my friends, co-workers, and support system that are too numerous to name, you are amazing! Where would I be without all of you? Your constant encouragement and excitement have meant the world to me. Kisses upon kisses to my launch team for helping get the word out and for your willingness to partner with this vision. Special thanks to Darla Hall for always believing in the dreams of others and for using your gift of photography to capture meaningful moments in my family and for me. Britt Silcox, thank you for your creative website design gifting, encouragement and for talking me off the ledge of discouragement and doubt time and time again. You always have the best timing! Pastor Rusty and Leisa, my church covering and home, thank you for the breath of fresh air that I will never forget when I walked in the doors seventeen years ago. God has done so much in my life through you and will continue to. For that I am eternally grateful. For all those who gave endorsements and even considered reading this manuscript, Pastor Laura Lee, Evangelist Curtis Silcox, Evangelist Sean Smith, and others, I am so grateful for your words, and thank you for taking the time out to read and cheer me on.

Very important thanks go to my family. Sometimes I can hardly believe that I get to do life with the most beautiful and feisty people I know. I'm so thankful for the heritage that God has allowed to be my story. To my Icelandic family in-love, you are some of the kindest and most generous people I have ever met. It's so wonderful to have such love and support from all of you. Daddy, thank you for challenging us and pushing us to be better and to work harder. I know my love of books and writing comes from you. Chima (Sampson), you will always be my baby brother, and I am so proud of the man you have become. I love seeing you walk out your calling. Tori (Victoria), you are my favorite feisty and fierce sister. My best facial expressions come from you, and you make me laugh like no other. Junior (Christian), you are seriously one of the kindest men that I know. I love your heart and am thankful we navigated some of the hardest years together. Mommy. I have no words for how thankful I am that God chose me to be your daughter. You gave me my best gift. An environment that set me on a course to know Jesus, truly and deeply. You are the Naomi in my life that showed me Christ even in your darkest moments. You are the best mother any child could ask for, and what a blessing it is to say that you are the best grandmother any child could ask for too!

To my children, Nyema (my warrior princess), Thor (my compassionate warrior prince), and Eyja (my prophetic princess), you are the greatest gifts, the picture of the faithfulness and generosity of God to me. I am so thankful to be your mom. Thank you for letting Momma write this book, even when I had to be locked in my room, hidden upstairs, or typing feverishly into my phone while you slept in my arms. My heart and my love are for my husband, Bjarni Thor. The fanner into flame of my dreams, my encourager who constantly prodded me about finishing this book until I gave up my objections and excuses and did so. Your pursuit of me and your constant pursuit of God challenge me to move further, to get closer, to dig deeper. I love you. Thank you for loving me and our children so well. Thank you for setting Christ as the center of our home. The best is yet to come.

Lastly, because He is the most important, Jesus, thank you for loving me. For dying on the cross, for rising again, for choosing me to be yours. You caused a five-year-old to fall deeply in love with you, and she has never been the same. She never wants to be the same. You know this is all for you, really it is. This is my perfume poured out at your feet in brokenness and thankfulness that you know me by name, that you call me your own. I don't want to ever be without you. All my life is yours.

Undone,

Jenny Erlingsson

# Contents

# *Foreword*

"I love that in the Bible there seem to be many stories of unsuspecting women who make a huge difference. Or at least for us if we were to meet them face to face, we would never suspect the potential that is beneath their surface" (Chapter 8—Jael).

*'Becoming His'* is a journey that began for all of us the moment we breathed our first breath: *"All the days ordained for me were written in your book before one of them came to be"* (Psalm 139:16, NIV). All of my days, every one of them, from birth to death, was written about me in a novel HE took great care in writing before I ever gasped in the breath of God—and within this book is the epic story, our story, of *Becoming His*. Yes, your story is **epic**! It is miraculous; it is a "must-read" and a testimony that needs to be heard—not because it is perfect, with no sin, no trials, no wrong turns, but it is miraculous because, just like the lives of the women you are about to meet, He is woven into every moment. Even when there is doubt, hurt, loss, blessing, confusion, rebellion, sin, victory, and redemption, He is guiding us ever so gently, with the wind of His Spirit, as we walk out the pages of our story.

We are not much different than the women you are about to meet. As a matter of fact, it is my prayer that after this journey into His heart, you can add your name to this list of women. Remember, they are not qualified because their stories are in the Bible. They are qualified because they persevered through the journey of *Becoming His*. Our potential does not lie in what we see at the beginning of our journey, but what we become when the road is the roughest. Eve was the first lady of the divinely created, but she was also the one who first tasted of sin, first felt the pains of childbirth, and first experienced the loss of a child. Sarah laughed at God and took the matters of her promise into her own hands. Miriam, at a young age, knew her God so deeply as a slave and pressed past fear, making a way for her brother, the deliverer. God saw Rahab even in her sin. HE spoke and she listened; HE led and she followed, and her people were saved. Jael was nothing more than a hammer-wielding warrior woman—ignoring the taunt of the enemy and choosing to be God's secret weapon. Ruth pressed past her loss and her loneliness and chose to honor—an unwavering commitment, which made way for the lineage of King David. And Hannah…after years of empty arms, longing for the gift of a child, when her arms were finally full and her heart overflowing—she gave this son back to the Lord—the greatest offering…all she had to give.

Oh, the "unsuspecting potential" that has been growing within the depths of who you are! It's HIStory, being told through the pages of your life, just like these women. In the tough years, the broken moments, and the questions…HE IS THERE. In the confusion, the wrong turns, the victories, and the triumphs…HE IS THERE. In the moments of despair and the valley of doubt…HE IS THERE. And it is for this reason you have to *know* that HE IS FOR YOU! And His greatest joy is for you to know Him and for you to know that YOU ARE HIS! Believing in who you are cannot be attained until you truly *know* you are His. HE made this possible because of the Cross of Calvary:

- He was forsaken so I could walk in freedom.

- He was left alone so I could be lead always.

- He was rejected so I could be made righteous.

- He was abandoned so that I could be atoned.

- He was deserted so I could have dominion.

- He was ignored so i could know an indescribable God.

In 1999, I began a new chapter in my story with my husband. We left the state of Florida where we had served for over fifteen years as youth pastors, college pastors, worship leaders, and, for our final five years in Florida, executive pastors. This new journey was not only bringing us home to North Alabama, but also throwing us into planting a church and picking up the mantle of becoming lead pastors. During that first year, as the church grew, as He was "adding to the church daily" and multiplying our congregation supernaturally, families began walking beside us, carrying the vision and making covenant with what He had birthed in our hearts.

One such family was the Enyindas: Patience, a single mom from Nigeria—who, to this day, is one of my heroes—and her four amazing children, Jenny, Chris, Victoria, and Chima.

Since then, I have had the privilege of not only seeing these children grow up, but the honor of being part of their lives. The eldest of the four, Jenny, is your writer and your navigator, the one who will open up a portion of His heart for you in the pages of this book. It is not my intention for this to sound like a bio; rather, it is—out of complete love for her journey—a heart-felt desire for you to catch a tiny glimpse into her pursuit of Him.

Jenny graduated high school about two years after I met her family. She graduated from the University of Tennessee and earned her Masters degree from Alabama A&M University shortly thereafter. Through her college years, I watched her dedication, her perseverance, and her commitment, all the while staying connected to her home church, loving and honoring her mother, and being the most amazing big sister anyone could ask for.

After pursuing and completing her education, Jenny returned home, working for eight years as our church's junior high youth pastor and pursuing grants. She has always excelled in all she has put her hands to, and honestly, I could fill even more pages of this book with her abilities, her passions, her gifts, and how loved she is by all. For me, this confirms one of the greatest assets and privileges of being a pastor—and that is raising up daughters, living your life before them, nurturing them to embrace their journey, helping them find their wings, and watching them fly. Over the past seventeen years, I have been in the grandstands with countless others witnessing Jenny becoming His! And for the past three years, I have had a front row seat—because she is my assistant, and she is my friend.

I invite you to plunge yourself into the pages of this book and into the lives of these women—not fictional women, but real women, just like you and just like me. Don't miss a word! Position yourself to hear Him intimately. Jenny has captured the key to a portal, which will lead us into a place within His heart few will ever know they can visit.

—Leisa Nelson
Senior Pastor, along with her husband, Rusty,
The Rock Family Worship Center,
Huntsville, Alabama

# Introduction

This is about the journey to remember who we are and to whom we belong. All of us as women have one thing in common no matter our life circumstance. We may not have siblings, husbands, children, or grandchildren, but we were all born. We are all daughters. And that core position is the central theme of this book. Contained within these pages are stories of our sisters. Women of the faith who have gone before us. They didn't necessarily get it right all the time and they didn't always have it so bad either. The key here is not the measure of their success but that they went *before*. They form the cloud of witnesses pressing us on, encouraging, speaking life over us because they now dwell in the presence of *true* life. Their stories as told in scripture remind us that they had parts to play in HIStory; they made their mark somehow for His glory. What we read about them has both personal impact and prophetic implications for our lives and the world.

Or maybe just for you, as your fingers thumb through the snippets and snapshots of the lives that are highlighted—maybe the impact and implication is just for you. That's how it's been for me. It is not my desire nor intention to add to the Word of God through the imaginative expressions of the stories that are shared. But because of what I know of our Father's heart and guiding of the Holy Spirit, I see these women not just in the black and white context of the text but fleshed out beautifully in the colors and personalities that God gave them, the impact of their responses to the circumstances set before them, the mistakes they made…the way they lived their lives. And I have to believe that even the ones who seemed to fail miserably did not necessarily have to be destined to a bad ending. We don't get to read in depth about the end of all of their lives, especially after a crisis. But I believe it's because the Lord wants us to consistently go to Him for the answers, to dig deeper and let Him continue the stories on the pages of our hearts. To write those meaningful endings and beginnings into our own lives.

And after it all there may be just one word or phrase that you take with you…or none at all. You see, to me that *is* beautiful. Because all this randomness comes together in a lovely fragrance that I hope draws you into deeper relationship with Jesus and also ministers to Him. It is a box broken, a perfume poured out, a response to a price that He has paid for us. It is the spices and flowers and seeds and fruits crushed together to form an oil that lingers, a scent that reminds us that when it all comes down to it, we are His in all of our complexities, quirks, weaknesses, strengths, laughter, and mourning. So read wide open; take what you will and what you need, but remember it's all just meant to point you back to Him. To remind you, my sister, that we are His and that's all that matters.

# PART 1

>>→

# His in the Beginning

She is made—carefully, intricately woven into the masterpiece that He would call mankind. A kind of wonderful that would be like no other creature. She was made like no other but made for another, not as a problem to be handled but as a solution, as an answer. A response to a longing previously unfulfilled, a kiss, a thrill of excitement and joy, as she touches down, girl meets boy, boy meets joy, meets the expression of divine that he couldn't quite articulate until he saw this Eve, his mate. This mother. This dancer. This serenade of creation. A lullaby of love and provision from their maker. She was made. In His image to represent His image, to birth His image, populate the earth with His image, to join in the reproduction of His very presence. She was made as His melody over the earth, a balm after a day's work, to sing of beauty and worth, the laughter and the mirth; she was made perfect and lovely, not a flaw marred her features, but to Him she was the standard of loveliness, a work of art in moving form. Poetry in motion, how she must have danced, run, soared, beautiful feet…lifting, swaying, hopping, playing to eternity's rhythm. She was made to fit him. Partner for life to dwell beside, a companion she was made. She had not earned and so did not deserve such favor, yet...there was one who would make it seem so. One who would twist words once spoken into barbs of half-truths that would pull her through, discarding the gift that was given for that which they wanted to take. Grasping for temporary satisfaction in exchange for eternal relationship, she reached out for that which was forbidden and forgot she was made. So she gave lies a way, so she gave blame a name, so she hid from her source of wonder and forgot that she was made. And her identity as a solution became a problem that would plague. But she was still made and no mistake could erase the divine original intent of the Creator and the promises He conveyed, a promise that before she was formed He had made. For already there was one who was the lamb that was slain. He promised that from her brokenness, beauty He would make.

# 1

# Eve

>>→

## PROFILE

I don't know what it means or even how to describe it. But I feel wind within me, an exhale…I inhale all of it. It comes within and without bouncing around every part of me until I feel it in every space I didn't know existed. It's vibrating through my senses, a gentle hum stirring me to wake. It is food and water, light and sound, exhilaration and peace…yes, peace. A knowing that everything is as it should be and here I am, separated and connected to the source of that breath…breath, ahh…that's what it is. I feel more of its warmth on my face, closer, deeper. My eyes open to infinite color. I am in the center of a gaze, and it is unbearable beauty yet I cannot look away. He says my name. I close my eyes to ponder and savor; all at once I am empowered and uncovered. I am His and He is mine. My eyes open again and this time they are assaulted by wonder. That's what I call it—wonder, staring at me. And this time, instead of eternal orbs I see an image reflected back at me in the center of this gaze. The color deep, rich, like the fire I feel in me.

I am awake.

He stands before me. I don't know him, but somehow I know he is mine. The same breath I know flows through his body, linking us in a way that should not be broken. He takes my hand, that thing that opens and closes at the end of a long and graceful extension of me. Me. That is who I am. Not just the breath or vibration I feel but a form that is standing carefully as he pulls me to what I am soon to call feet. He takes me into his matching arms and holds me close, a beat pounding against my chest that I cannot determine the source of. He holds me close as if to take all of me into him and I do the same, studying him with every cell of my body. I am his and he is mine.

He teaches me much, this Adam of mine. This man, this ruler of all that is before us. He shows me the rolling of the hills, the clear blue of the rivers that flow through our garden, the intelligence of the animals that serve as our companions. The intricate detail of their ways is mesmerizing, from the flit of the hummingbird to the smooth stride of the cheetah. And he shows me the ways we are so perfectly fit together, my Adam and I. I know every part of him as he knows of me. But more wondrous than all these are those moments when the atmosphere of the garden stands still, the very mist parts, and the animals bow. When in the most beautiful and serene part of the day, the very maker of it all comes in. He is everywhere and around everything in an instant, yet we behold Him as He stands with us, as close as our very breath. He is the breath, the wind that brings substance to our form, and we await His coming with anticipation.

There is so much more of Him that I desire and yet so much I do not know. Adam answers questions for me as much as he can; he speaks to me of the words spoken to him even before I was created.

All things are at our fingertips, all for our taking except, mysteriously, for one thing.

This one, I admit I look at rather often. Although I try to keep my gaze away, when I am near there is an attraction that I can only compare to when our maker is near. Yet this one gnaws at me and draws me closer. I see the workings of the One in all that He has made and I long to understand how this tree represents Him as well. Even the animals who have roamed this place longer than I don't seem to know, nor do they seem to care. They are content in their roles, happy in their doings, all except for one. And I see that he joins me this day as I gaze at the tree. I sense my Adam coming near, and I sense this creature coming closer. And as Adam joins my side, the tree filling our minds' eyes, the voice of the serpent starts to whisper, "Did God actually say...?"

His words begin to weave webs of thought and question, the burden of it all pressing in our minds until we crave a release of the pressure. I sense the longing in my Adam as strongly as I feel it in myself. Surely if everything in the garden is good this one thing has to be as well. I remember the words shared, the command given to my husband that he passed along to me. But perhaps that was for the beginning; surely it could not mean for always. Why would our maker withhold anything from us that would be good? Even as I ponder I feel the slight shiver of surrender. I want to know more, and to think I could know it now stirs up a strange pleasure. "Eve?" I hear my name in hesitation, I hear it in doubt, and as I turn to the source I see that Adam is farther behind me now. The direction of my thoughts led me closer to that which I wanted to be closer to, I wanted to partake of its fruit. And my Adam, I know, has wanted to taste it too.

I reach carefully for the fruit, no fear in my approach, yet a twinge of something I do not quite understand appears on the inside of me. I look back again to Adam, expecting him to give me a reason to turn away. But the look in his eyes urges me forward. He is unsure but the desire to define the unknown overrides what he knows. I turn back to my task and reach up ever so slightly to take hold of that fruit. As I grasp its flesh I hear a slight hissing on the wind, almost as if the serpent creature laughs. I take a bite and oh... my eyes, it is almost too bright; slightly blinded I give Adam the fruit to taste. He too takes a bite and immediately shields his eyes. After the light dims I blink, looking around to see that everything has been made more dull...and quiet. I did not realize how much the music in our garden colored our senses with vibrant, decadent hues. We were to see more clearly; we were to know what we did not. Yet what I see leaves me wanting; what I know is disconcerting. The world as I know it has lost its color, and somehow I know that it is changed forever.

# PONDER

Have you ever had a craving? Had a taste for something so strong that it filled your thoughts when you let your mind roam freely? Something that diverted your attention and made you lose focus? I have and I do, all the time. There is some good that I have the intention of doing, but then again I don't want to do it because what I crave seems so much sweeter in the moment than what I'm trying to move toward. It seems silly that the things that are so glaringly temporary steal our focus off of what is meant to remain in our lives.

So here it is, my confession. At this moment I have the strongest craving for a big, flavorful, juicy, taste-the-rainbow bag of...Skittles. Skittles? Yes, you heard me correct. You probably think I am crazy and making up some strange confession for the sake of illustration. Truth be told, that may come later in this book, but I speak honestly when I say this—I am addicted to candy. And I guess it wouldn't be so bad if I hadn't just come out of a time of fasting when I laid down those treats. Not to mention I didn't eat candy for three years in a commitment to praying and waiting for my future husband. Yet there are days I may be found rummaging through my children's lunch boxes for leftover fruit snacks. Candy is oftentimes my trade. It is my weakness.

Before you close this book and pick up the magazine you really wanted to read or the Instagram update that might catch your interest, give me a few minutes. I didn't put all these words down to talk about a 12-step program to be freed from candy addiction (although if there is one of that nature it might behoove me to be a part). There is something more important for both you and me to understand and learn. There is a transformation of thought that must occur in our lives in order for our words, feelings, actions, habits, and lifestyles to change. We must exchange the lies we have believed and the counterfeits we've clung to for the fullness of life that God intended us to have. And for me at times it starts with candy and leads to a lack of self-control, a need for comfort and quick satisfaction, a deficit in my trust in the Lord. Where does it start for you?

For Eve, it started with a voice. A word, a whisper, a command. We don't know if Eve heard the rule with her own two ears, but we can be sure she knew of it. In the biblical fiction book *Havah*[1], author Tosca Lee speculates so beautifully that maybe Adam had received the command before Eve was formed and therefore Eve did not hear it directly from God himself, although it did not diminish its relevance to her. The Bible says that Eve was *deceived*. Basically, she was led to believe something that was not true. This is not to direct all blame away from her or justify her actions. And by actions I mean that incident of fruit sampling that took place among our freshly formed ancestors. Through the coaxing of the serpent-clothed Satan, Eve was influenced to grab a hold of that which was forbidden in order to receive what she craved. And whether or not she heard God say the words was not the issue; the issue was obedience. This was the first test of humanity.

When we delve deeper into the dynamics of this story we realize that this is more than a children's Bible illustration. Two main questions come up when we dissect what was taking place—two out of the mass of thoughts I have, like, "Did Adam have a belly button?" "Could they talk to animals?" "Were they vegetarians?" or "Why, oh, why did pains in childbirth have to be increased?!" Out of all those irrelevant thoughts my core questions are these:

1. Why did Eve (and Adam) choose to listen to the voice of the enemy instead of God?

2. Why didn't Eve (and Adam) just ask God for knowledge?

I mean, they had contact with the Creator of the universe. The one who breathed out the very stars spent the lush evenings conversing with them, sharing His presence with them, allowing them to know Him. And yet the voice of the unfamiliar began to echo some deep desires of their hearts, and they decided to follow a voice that justified what their cravings were. Ugh...sound familiar? God had already spoken and made it clear what His desire was for Adam and Eve, yet they were influenced by another voice. I can only imagine that as time passed in the garden they frequented the place where that tree was. Their indifference turning to curiosity, curiosity into interest, and interest into a craving. And the enemy knew. He noticed the subtle changes in their behavior, the growing pull of their attraction, and he took advantage of the moments he had to begin to plant words that sounded right in their ears. And I say "their" because, according to scripture, it wasn't just Eve standing there alone. The Bible says that Adam was *with her* when he took the fruit from her hand.

So why did they choose to listen to this other voice? Maybe because they hadn't allowed the voice of God to reign supreme in their lives. Maybe instead of rehearsing God's purpose and promises even when they didn't understand, they leaned on their own understanding and began to dwell on what they didn't have. In doing so, they exchanged the truth of God for a lie because in that instance the lie seemed to be more valuable, to hold more weight. And that is where we find ourselves time and time again—the battle between what has been said, because *it is* what has been promised, and then what is before our eyes as a temporary satisfaction.

That's what it always is, isn't it? Temporary, not lasting, like a vapor—our satisfaction. We throw all our resources toward things that really don't mean a drop in the bucket when it comes to eternity. We search the Internet, books, and friends for the things we need to fulfill us when the true source is as close as our very breath, as intimate as our spirit. *If* we've chosen He who chose us first. Yet we don't go to Him, at least not always first. In Jeremiah 33:3, God gives us this beautiful promise that I don't think we always fully grasp. In it He says, *"call to me and I will answer you, and will tell you great and hidden things that you have not known"* (NRSV). There is so much powerful beauty in this verse. I will do my best to unpack it for you, but I don't want the simple magnitude of it to be complicated either. So consider that first He says "call." We could end it all right there. The fact that I have permission to call on Him is mind blowing. We have access to the one who breathed the stars out, the one who spoke a word and things came to be. The one who has such vast authority yet He says *call to Me*—so poignant, so personal His beckoning. We get to be friends with God. It is this very friendship we were created for. The type that Adam and Eve were allowed to walk in before they made that dreadful exchange.

As we continue in this verse, God then says, "I will answer you"—not another person, not an angel, but He, He himself personally will answer our call to Him. Many of us stop here because when we hear that God will answer us we automatically assume that He will answer our prayer. That He will give us exactly what we have been asking for. He may do that, or He may just say, "Yes, darling, I'm listening." Both are so tremendously valuable, and I think we can honestly say that the latter may be worth more than the former. The Creator of the universe is saying that He will answer us each and every time.

I can't say that I answer my daughter each time she calls for me. Many times I am tired of her questions; I grow weary of her repetition. I at times choose to ignore because I have already told her what she wants to hear or I respond with probably more attitude than I intend to. I believe at times that my daughter's chatter is legitimate, but I think that most of the time she bounces her incessant words off of me in order to just remind herself that I am hers and that I and her daddy are the source of her knowledge. Parenthood has been the best picture of the nature of the Father toward me. He says that when I call to Him and ask Him my sometimes legitimate, but mostly repetitious, annoying, doubtful, incessant, excessive questions He will answer me! *Although God answers what we ask of Him, those answers are not more important than the answerer. My hope is that in this life more than His presents—I crave His presence.* I'm pretty sure I fail daily, but that is what I'm moving toward.

This verse has already proven awesome, but then He says, "and will tell you great and hidden things that you have not known." So not only is He saying I can call Him, not only is He saying He will answer, but then He has the almighty audacity to say that He will tell us even more things that we could never imagine or even know how to ask for. Secrets and mysteries, insight and intimacies, if we simply use the key of *call*.

So...when I consider Eve and all that was lost, I wonder why she didn't just ask. Why she didn't take hold of what was offered her. I know, of course, she didn't have the Holy Spirit-inspired words of Jeremiah before her as we do now, the ability to look through scriptures and dig out promises. But sister, she had the King of kings walking with her daily in the cool of the day, in the quietest moments when she could lay her heart bare. She was made for relationship with Him, and in that relationship He would not have withheld any good thing from her. Yet…here we are, made for the same relationship, given the same opportunity through Jesus.. Not with a tree in front of us but many more desirable, entangling, temporary things. Our choice must be made in the smallest and largest of ways, in minute details and major decisions. And there is a God who beckons us, gives us permission to call to Him, to be saturated in His voice and His alone, and to hear the secrets of His heart that outweigh any temporary thing. He's listening.

## PRESS IN

1. What was or could have been Eve's strength?

2. What was or could have been her weakness?

3. What is the biggest thing she needed to grasp during this time of beginnings?

4. What is the Holy Spirit saying to you about being His through Eve's story?

# 2

# Noah's Wife

>>→

GENESIS 6:9–8:22

## PROFILE

There is silence. I cannot tell if I am relieved or terrified. The sounds had all been so loud, so piercing, so deafening that now in silence I sit in shock. I barely feel the bodies of my children huddled next to me, their adulthood dwarfed by the intensity of this moment. They stick close to me as they did when they were barely weaned. Sons and wives shuddering and shaking, too afraid themselves to make a noise. I don't know if this is how we imagined it would be. Did we even think this would truly be a reality? The challenge and adventure of His command filled our every waking moment; the sounds of our progress served as the soundtrack to our lives. For so many years, for so many nights shouts of doubt, disbelief, incredulity, and hate were thrown at us. Yet still we pressed on, still we moved toward what we were told was to come, but we underestimated the depth, the true weight of promise. Now here we are in what our hands have built, and after all the weeping and

*are they talking about the Ark? If so, this was a scary experience?*

*pretty sure its the ark ♥*

*(handwritten margin note: yup. Definitely the Ark.)*

wailing, the scratching and beating, there is silence. The sound of a world that has been drowned out. Why did it have to come to this? And why, oh why did it come to us? Surely we are not worthy. Was I more righteous than those who did not make it on this ship? Am I truly thankful to have been saved or more terrified of what is to come?

I look over to my husband, the one out of all others I have made covenant with. This was the first of my many foolish choices according to my family. How could I settle for just one man when there was opportunity to taste of all humanity had to offer? How could he settle for just me? To others it was such a strange choice when there were many other women vying for his attention, ready to give him anything he desired. They had been set on turning his head and heart. Yet he chose me. As I look over at him, huddled in a corner, the weight of all that has happened on his shoulders, I can't help but be thankful. I never thought I had much to give, even when I gave him my hand in covenant, even when midwives handed him our infant boys on the days of their births, even when I brought food and water to him and our sons as they beat this boat out of gopher wood and tar. But now I realize that there is so much more I have the opportunity to do.

The task was not complete when we finished building the instrument of our rescue. When this is all over we must build a world with not just our hands but our bodies, our sweat, our lives. We shall be the foundation of a new world, and all I can see are the cracks in me, the flaws that deem me not worthy. Yet here I am, floating, covered, rescued, mother to my shaking children, wife to my trusting husband, daughter to the Creator of this water-saturated world.

There may not be much of me left when it is all said and done, but I *can* give the fullness of my support and encouragement. I can remind my Noah that even amidst all the devastation and horror of what has happened, there is a light of hope found in the eyes of his sons, in the eyes of their wives who will produce even more sons and daughters. I can help take the words he receives from our God and continue to engrain them in our offspring, teach them to my children's children, letting a pure love for the Creator pass from generation to generation. I swallow the threatening sobs, the sorrow that is thick in my throat. I can help prevent the type of destruction that has swept away my own generation. For I was not only chosen by my husband, but his God, my God, chose me.

I carefully release myself from my children and stand shaking, doing my best to move with the sway of the boat as I make my way toward him. I hear his weeping as I get closer, his rare heart of obedience and compassion untainted by the years of his existence on the hard earth we once knew. I know that he grieves for those who are lost, for the ones who would not put aside their pride and the lust of their flesh to make the decision to believe and come. I know that if he could he would have given his life if only they had come. I kneel down beside him and surround him with my arms, pulling him into my embrace. I don't know what will become of us truly, but I can do my best to love him, this man I've been given, even in the midst of uncertainty. And when doubts come and fear tries to linger, I will remind him and our children of the one by whose hands we have been saved.

# PONDER

We sat across from each other at a certain hamburger restaurant. We were beginning a relationship that I had prayed about for what seemed like all my life. I had pictured many scenarios in my head when it came to marriage, but I don't know if I had seen it quite like this. Now granted, we were not necessarily talking about marriage then, but the words we spoke that day I will never forget. Because my soon-to-be husband was not promising me a life full of ease or comfort but wanted to make sure that I knew that even though what he did in his work may look like a romantic adventure there was also a reality to it. He didn't just minister in the inner areas of our city or to those struggling with a variety of issues. He lived in the midst, he took care of needs in his home, and he gave himself more than 100 percent to what God had given him to do in that season. He wanted to make sure I knew fully, I guess, so that I could jump ship before we moved farther down the road together. However, I was not planning on going anywhere anytime soon. I don't know what gave me the boldness or faith to do so, but I assured him that I'd always known my life would be an adventure and that's the way I wanted it.

Fast forward to a couple years later and me at the center of a small home with five children I did not give birth to and one little girl who had come from my womb. There were days when the weariness was almost too much to handle or when my hormones were turning me into a crazy mama bear type creature. I know for certain that my response was not always perfect or polite or sweetened with grace, but somehow I was determined to live up to what I had promised. I was and am in covenant with my husband, through the good and bad, health and sickness, and even in crazy obedience to God. Because the Lord had called us and caused us to be joined together, I now had a large part to play in the destiny that was purposed for my husband. In the same way, my husband also would be intertwined with what God had called me to do. The purposes and plans God has for our lives were meant to be merged into one.

We read the tale of Noah and sometimes skip over all the players who were involved in this story. Not to get all preachy up in here, but just because someone doesn't have a name doesn't mean they don't have a story. Or even truer, just because you don't know someone's name doesn't mean they don't have one. Our God knows exactly what He is doing in and through the lives of people even if we do not. This was so very true even in what we read about Noah. His story takes place numerous years after the incident of the garden. To sum it all up, the world has fallen into such a state of disarray that the next plan of action is for everyone to be wiped out. Except for a faithful few.

Even amidst our lack of understanding of why this course of action had to be, we need to understand that it was. Even research tells us that most of the major creation myths and stories of the world have a flood in them. This cataclysmic event was the catalyst to a new world, and it was seen through the eyes of not just Noah but of the people who surrounded him in the ark. Noah's wife is not known by name to us, but she must be known. Even if she had her own set of fears she was a willing participant in what took place or she would have been one of the many swept away with the waters. I can't imagine her emotions as she heard from her husband what God was planning to do. Disbelief, fear, anger, sadness, regret, hesitation, who knows? We can only know by looking in ourselves and dissecting how we react when we are given news of such huge change. It doesn't have to come from the mouth of our spouse; it may be from parents, employers, friends, or those in authority over us. It may even be the report of a doctor that shakes us to the core.

When these instances come it may be easier to drown in our questions than to walk fully into the obedience that is asked of us. Especially when the decisions are not originating from ourselves but from someone we trust. But if we are ones who do trust in Jesus as Lord over our lives, then we must trust that even in the circumstances we don't understand there is a response that we are responsible for. There is something that we have to give, something that we are being trusted with.

Most might overlook Noah's wife, especially as she is nameless in the Word. The beautiful part of this story is that she wasn't nameless to God. And in the great mandate that Noah was given, she needed to be in place to give her full support and encouragement. I wonder how many nights Noah might have wanted to give up or give in, to go with the flow of what was about to take place rather than continue building this structure that was such an affront and offense to the people around them. Someone had to be the encourager; someone had to remind him of the words that had been spoken from their Creator. Noah's wife wasn't just joined to him to be a producer of his children; she played an integral part in carrying out of the call that God had given.

After their time in the boat, they were given a promise and then a command. In Genesis 9:7 He said, *"As for you, be fruitful and increase in number; multiply on the earth and increase upon it."* Noah's wife obviously had a very central role in the fruitful and multiplication part, as did the wives of her sons. Yet, we cannot forget that she had a keen awareness of what caused the "decrease" of people on the earth. She would now be responsible for setting the course of sustained fruitfulness and moral multiplication. In short, she had the responsibility of helping her husband set the atmosphere for the world as they knew it. She needed to help teach her children and their offspring how they could continue to be blameless and walk faithfully with the Lord as Noah had. That doesn't mean mistakes would not be made. We read about some immediate ones as we go further in the story. You and I have also both lived long enough to know that mistakes are made daily by all of us who have increased upon this earth. Even so, the role of Noah's wife wasn't any less significant. She was such a valuable part of all that would play out.

In the midst of such upheaval, we cannot underestimate our role within the circumstances that God has trusted us with. In every situation we cannot forget that God has not just placed people in *our* lives, but we've also been placed in theirs. When we are surrounded by truly godly relationships there is a beautiful reciprocity that should be taking place. Encouraging each other, helping one another to remain faithful and obedient, providing the resources that we have stewardship of to help support. And in every relationship, with all types of people you may be the shoulder to cry on when it's needed, answering questions as honestly as you can, being honest with your own questions as they come. Because God is trusting you not only with the destiny He's given you but with the ones He has amazingly intertwined with others in your life. At times you may be unnamed, seemingly insignificant, or without any apparent value, but oh, sister, you are valuable and more. You can be a source of peace, of encouragement, of resource, of life to those God has placed in your sphere of influence. Making the decision to stand for what is truthful and godly, even when there is insurmountable opposition. Operating in compassion until the end, even when others choose not to be chosen. When all the world turns against, you may be the one who places a hand at the small of a generation's back, surrounding them with your embrace, pressing them forward into the destiny God is calling them to.

*Remember:* (handwritten margin note)

# PRESS IN

1. What was or could have been Noah's wife's strength?

2. What was or could have been her weakness?

3. What is the biggest thing she needed to grasp during this time of beginnings?

4. What is the Holy Spirit saying to you about being His through the story of Noah's wife?

# 3

# Sarah

>>→

Genesis 18:1–15
(also Genesis 12:10–20, Genesis 15–17,
Genesis 20:1–18 for further study)

## PROFILE

Sweat trickles down my back as I rest in the shade of my tent. It is the hottest part of the day, and the only reasonable thing to do is to rest. If that is what I can call it. There seems to never be any rest for me. The years have taken me down paths I never imagined or wanted. I've longed for things, longed for answers I never seem to receive. What good is a body at rest whose mind cannot? I replay many moments in my head, especially on days like this when the sweltering heat beats down on my senses and brings mirages even to the mind's eye. Yet, these mirages are more than faded memory, they are constant reminders that still leave me in the grip of fear. Lies and capture, harems and release. Doubt and offers, jealousy and…

I turn my head slightly at the sound of laughter. Only the young seem to enjoy themselves in weather like this. Especially this one, with laughter like his father. The twinge of familiar pain causes me to sit up a little more, as if my movement will bring some alleviation from the pain of grief. I am a woman torn, wavering between my emotions. It is not that I wish he was not here. He is handsome and strong, the picture of beautiful youth. Yet, with all my good intentions I never intended to feel this way. As if a piece of my heart was torn out, my greatest hope morphed into a constant fear. Fear to miss out, fear of never experiencing, fear to be lied about and given up again.

I sigh and shift closer to the fan my servant waves over me. The cool breeze it generates the only relief on this day. Suddenly she stops and I glance up to see what has caused her hesitation. With wide eyes she looks in shock out of the tent. "What is it?" I don't know if I am more irritated at the halt of my breeze or more interested to have something break up my mood. "My lady, it is my lord. He is… running?" That in itself is enough to move me out of my position. I take her hand to stand up and feel the bubble of laughter within me. I still have the ability to move about quite well and could move even briskly if I needed to, but never in the past ten years have I seen my husband run. The sight of his hurry brings a strange joy and a single tear to my eye.

As he gets closer I call out, "What is it, husband? What has caused your great haste?" Not even his son Ishmael distracts him as he heads into my tent. "Quick," he breathes, "get some of your best flour and knead it and bake some bread." Before I can even say anything he takes off again toward the herd. He himself begins to move through the animals looking for, I'm sure, the best calf. If he wants me above all the servants to make bread, there must be someone important headed our way.

I notice a group of men sitting at the great trees that stand near Abraham's tent. As I squint my eyes to get a better look, the one in the middle stands up. He raises his hand slightly as if to wave and nods his head with a smile. The more I look, the more he comes into focus. I see him with the eyes of my youth, and for a moment time stands still and swirls around this familiar stranger and I. I feel as if he knows me like no one else does—not Abraham, not like those kings of the past tried to, not like my father or mother, not like anyone I have ever met. Yet, I am not afraid. I blink and the picture of the men to my eye regains the blur of distance. I shake myself of my reverie and go to prepare for my task.

After everything is prepared and set before the men, I decide to stay around the entrance to my husband's tent. These strangers and the way my husband is acting around them is raising my curiosity. They eat in comfortable silence for a while under the tree, a few words here and there when Abraham asks how they are enjoying the weather, or their journey, or the food. When he asks of my bread I hear one of them say, "Speaking of your wife, where is she?" "There in the tent," he says, pointing back to me. Instinctively, I move further into his tent. He continues speaking without turning his head to look back at me. "I will surely return to you about this time next year, and Sarah your wife will have a son."

The men have left, two in the direction of Sodom and Gomorrah, the one and Abraham on a walk in another direction. It is too late to retrieve my response, too late to grasp for what I released without thinking. Or is that even the truth? Do my own thoughts deceive me? For out of the overflow of the disbelief in my heart this, *this* comes out? In front of him? He calls my name and my first response is shame, so I try to deny what I've allowed to fly out. I laughed, a choking one, not believing that what this man said could be possible. A son. A son?! It is incredible that he thinks anything could come from me. I who have watched hope rise and wane, trying and trying, yet in vain. Longing for a promise, longing to name, and when he gives me a glimmer of hope my only refrain…is to laugh. The incredulity of it has caused me to lose my mind and all sense of decorum. I should not have even been listening.

Yet these are faithful words even to my own unfaithfulness, and he says again a gift shall come my way. My way in his way. It is too precious for words, the hope itself dangerous. I don't want to fall again, fall in love with seasons and what ifs and dreams again. To watch them dry up and pass unseasoned with fruitfulness and life. Yet here I stand, this laughing wife, told that nothing is impossible and that I will bear a promise. I in my old age will carry and give birth to a son. I don't dare to believe, but I don't desire to remain locked in my doubt any longer. I know all too well the consequences of wavering faith. Living beneath the full potential of what I had been promised opened the door to compromise, and I don't want to go to that place again. I don't want the fear or jealousy or rejection to fuel my life again and produce irrational thoughts. Faith in El Shaddai's ability to produce life in me is more of a reality than my cloudy disbelief. I will not linger in confusion and hesitation any longer. The laughter of disbelief *will* turn to one of joy.

# PONDER

I would have laughed too. Seriously. Even though Sarah, the wife of Abraham, hadn't experienced childbirth yet, I'm sure she had watched the process a few times. Helped in the delivery of relatives, servants, maybe a goat or two. And after having kids myself, I'm pretty sure that it is the hardest thing I've ever done, and between each child I always need time to forget the intensity of how each child was delivered if you know what I mean. I can understand why the concept was slightly hilarious and incredulous to her. Have a baby? At her age? With each passing year she probably had a harder time stooping to cook dinner, walking to the well without tripping over a rock, trying to hold down that same delivered goat to slaughter it for the evening meal much less give *birth!* For all she knew that would be the death of her. The desire to have a baby probably never waned, but to give birth…ha! She'd seen what that involved and that desire probably died the same time her ability to stay cool did. Hot flashes in the desert anyone? I mean no disrespect to the Lord and I'm sure neither did she.

But here is the simple truth: God has no parameter for His promises. He has no limit to how He can deliver them, pun intended. Sarah would be the mother to a new nation of people. That's what had been promised. In light of this, we may ponder in the safety of our 20/20 historical vision why she chose to give her servant Hagar to her husband to produce a son when she had already received a promise from God. A promise given *before* her encounter with the three men who were in reality two angels and the Lord Himself. Her situation seems unfathomable to us. When spouses have affairs there is so much pain in the process. Why would she willingly choose to put herself in that situation? She was the initiator of the relationship between her husband and Hagar.

Even though we may look at this in shock, the truth is that we are not that different in our decision-making. Maybe Sarah struggled like several of us do when we allow *who* we are to be defined by *what* we do. Therefore, when we feel like failures or deficient in the "doing" part we feel inadequate in the "being." Maybe she'd had enough of the whispering and murmuring directed toward her childlessness. Maybe she was still dealing with the residual rejection of almost being given up by her husband, twice. Because if he would reject her to a foreign king because of an area she excelled in, her *beauty*, then why would he not send her away for good for any area she was lacking in, like her *barrenness*? Even though she heard the promise before, somehow her circumstances outweighed those words and so…she gave Hagar into the hands of her husband. And maybe as she walked to that tent, a nervous Egyptian servant by her side, just maybe it was all a test for her husband. A way to be reassured, for him to reject her offer, draw her into his arms and calm her fears.

Fear of man is a dangerous thing; it can and will lead all of us into places we never thought we would go and into bitterness that can eat away at our souls. In this situation, fear opened the door for a counterfeit to enter their lives. This did not diminish Ishmael's value as the son of Abraham and Hagar. It did not mean that he was not loved by God. He was *very* loved. But for Abraham and Sarah it was not God's intention for him to carry out the specific promise intended to come through Isaac and specifically to come through her. Sarah allowed fear of man to motivate her to run ahead of God's promises and the significant place she had in them. Therefore she and her family had to deal with the consequences of those actions.

Fear of man. This does not mean that we crouch in the corner, sweating profusely when another member of the human race approaches us. It's not something that we may consider as strongly as other issues, but we must address it because I see it over and over again in women I meet, young and old. Every story is not the same, but a common theme runs through. With the absence, neglect, rejection, indifference, or even extreme expectations of an authority figure, especially a father, women are growing up with a strong performance mentality. It's not necessarily the urge to be the center of attention but to receive *some* attention, to please, to do everything right, to be noticed, to follow the rules, to be remembered. It is about seeking approval from others and therefore every action is dictated out of that need. When affirmation doesn't come, a multitude of emotions will—depression, anger, bitterness, insecurity, and more, more of the *doing* to try to feel worthy.

Sarah forgot that she was already a princess before she was a mother; before she was a wife she was already a daughter. She had allowed God's promise to illuminate her lack instead of highlight the goodness and faithfulness of God. Whatever pressure she had from society was shaping her into a woman moved by circumstance and therefore giving in to a temporary solution. Does this sound familiar? Ishmael wasn't an illegitimate child; God had a plan for him and his mother, but the plan was not for Sarah to circumvent the timing of God and go her own way in producing an heir for her husband. Unfortunately, she decided that the timing was in her hands and did what she thought was best to produce a child. This resulted in a firstborn who was not meant to receive firstborn promises and a nation that would be a constant struggle for Israel.

When we allow fear of man and, in turn, distrust of God to be our driving force, we give birth to fruit that was never meant to be a part of our lives. But when we understand who we belong to and that His timing is perfect, we can rest in the assurance that our value is not determined by what we perceive as our lack or even our abundance. Our value is set by Him. Think about it. Your Father in heaven is not swayed by the seeming delay of a promise. He stands outside of time. And guess what? He is the one who made the promise and is fully responsible for carrying it through. He's not just holding the world in his hands but also our past, present, and future. He sees the beginning and end result and is not moved by how long we think something is taking to happen. He is the God who ultimately has the first and last say-so, and He is also the one who can weave even all of our detours, mistakes, counterfeits, and temporary choices into a beautiful tapestry that reflects the fullness of His purposes. If we will let Him.

This hit me strongly about six years ago. It was a snippet, a blurb, not even a full message. But I stopped in my tracks and paid attention. Not just to the phrase going over and over in my head, but also to the leading of the Spirit in my heart saying, "Listen." I had just heard Lisa Bevere mention something in a promo video online for a conference. Her simple statement was this: "God's not into turns, He's into timing."

Timing…not turns. How simple yet profound! When we get this into our spirits, we move from little girls on the playground—fighting over their turn to swing, play with dolls, and be first in line—and into women who embrace the season in which God has them, confident in the work God is doing in them and through them and looking with expectancy to the timing God is bringing about. *"Let us not become weary in doing good, for at the proper time we will reap a harvest if we do not give up"* (Gal. 6:9). When this perspective becomes a part of our lifestyles, we drop the need to compare ourselves with one another because we realize that God is not withholding anything from us or blessing someone more than us. We don't have to dwell in insecurity or anxiety, waiting for our turn for whatever it is we are seeking. We can trust Him. He is our Father, the Writer of our story, and the Painter of the masterpiece that is you. We can trust that His timing always has been, always is, and always will be...perfect. And that we are and always will be *His*.

# PRESS IN

1. What was or could have been Sarah's strength?

2. What was or could have been her weakness?

3. What is the biggest thing she needed to grasp during this time of beginnings?

4. What is the Holy Spirit saying to you about being His through Sarah's story?

# 4

# Shiphrah and Puah (The Midwives)

>>→

Exodus 1:12–21

## PROFILE

We are dismissed. The finality of his statement is both intense and nonchalant. He has determined that what he has asked of us is the right decision and therefore will be carried out swiftly. He waves us away to move along with his next order of business. The trembling of our nerves has now turned to rolling waves of terror. We can barely lift our feet as we make our departure. For the first time in our lives we do not want to go home. We do not want to face the impossible choice that stands before us. We can't even look at each other. And there is no need. The grief that overwhelms our hearts will only be mirrored in each other's gaze. Our emotions are palpable. They fill our every step with heavy burden. How can everything change in an instant? One day, one decree, one word…

can change everything. The one thing that brings the most joy in the bleak world we live in will now be a constant source of sorrow.

Pain grips our hearts as we make our way, heads down, as if the news is written even in the sky. How can we even look in the eyes of our people when Pharaoh wants their children dead? How can we rejoice at new life knowing that we are to have a hand in that life's death? If they are male they are not allowed to exist. If female, they may live. But how will our race continue if there is no one to plant the seed? There will be no future, just women living in the sorrow of what has been lost. We will no longer be carriers of life but delivers of death. Our hands will be covered in the blood of our people.

There seems to be no escape from this awful fate...yet. We pause at the sound of a child's laugh coming from one of the homes we pass. So full of hope, so full of joy, unaware of the danger that lurks around the corner. The terror that is to come from our hands. Yet in that simple noise we hear the sound of more—we hear the call of generations waiting to be born, of redemption that will not be silenced. My sister and I face each other, tears streaming down our weary faces and we know...there is only one we obey, the only one who has sway over our lives. He is the only giver of life. Pharaoh does not have the power to give it, and he does not have permission to make us take it away.

Resignation takes its place in our hearts as fear gives way to love. We belong to someone greater than Pharaoh, and we will heed His ways for the Hebrew children. We will obey His voice alone. Consequences may come, but we will risk it all to give our people a chance. We smile for the first time in hours, our decision lifting the burden in our hearts. As our people trust us with the lives of their infants we will trust our God with our own and pray that He increases the people of Israel, despite the command of an earthly king. We will be with the mothers; we will help bring their babies to this world. And we will whisper in their untainted ears the truth of who they are.

# PONDER

In a society that demands tolerance and adherence to certain social cues, it can be hard to maintain the moral code that is instilled in us through our relationship with Christ. What is our response when we are faced with a dilemma of monumental proportions? What is our answer when we are seemingly forced to choose between a rock and a hard place? So many times it seems as if we are pitted against the world at large because of the nature of our beliefs, the ways that define the love affair we have with the King of the universe. And to a certain extent we *are* against certain agendas. When we get to the bottom of many of the worldly values that are presented to us on a daily basis, it is clear to see that there is a more sinister plan at work. One much deeper than what others think they are trying to convey. The Word of God says that the enemy comes to kill, steal, and destroy. This is so true in every aspect of the environment we live in now, and it was so true even thousands of years ago with a small developing nation called Israel.

The Bible doesn't say too much about Shiphrah and Puah, the midwives who stood in the presence of Pharaoh to receive his devastating command. But what is told about them speaks volumes of their character and their adherence to not the law of the day but the law that God had already written in their hearts. They were told to silence generations of Hebrews by killing the infant boys as they were born. Women who were meant to facilitate life were being told to have a hand in the death of a nation. They were between "a rock and a hard place" as we say so many times. And we say this phrase when the way out seems impossible. Did they dare go against the command of Pharaoh, who held their lives in his hand? Or would they go against the ways of their God who not only created and could take away their lives but had their souls in the palm of His hand?

For us looking in on the story the answer seems pretty clear cut. At least what we know to be right is obvious. Surely we would not stand by and allow innocent children to be killed all based on the command of an insecure and prideful king. Surely we too would choose the right path and not have a hand in destruction. However, this situation is not so farfetched when we think of what is allowed to take place in our current society. From abortion to sex trafficking, there are innocents being destroyed constantly and consistently. Where do we as followers of Christ stand in light of all of this? Our choice *should* be obvious. But some dilemmas don't always appear in our lives as absolutes. They may be choices that present themselves before us in subtler ways. Maybe it's choosing to remain pure and celibate in a relationship when all the world and our senses say to give in. Maybe it's deciding between a job you love and one that pays the bills. Maybe it's wondering if you really should place a foster child in your home or focus on the children you have already been given. Many times the choices are not so black and white, but myriads of gray with various potentials. And we wade through the process of decision-making hoping that God will yell down His answer from heaven so that our choice is made easier.

In my short life experience, however, I've found that many times the process to the decision is really the decision itself. The journey to what we are seeking oftentimes is the catalyst needed to strip off the ways and worries that were never meant to be ours. God may use the search for an answer as a way to position us to actually be at the place to receive that which we are seeking after. So instead of looking at the "rock and the hard place" and resigning ourselves to an impossible task, we need to stand on "the Rock" and position ourselves for a shift that allows us to see the hard place through the eyes and perspective of Christ, our solid rock.

He is the anchor that keeps us fastened to righteousness and holiness. We can't lean on excuses or shortcuts when we line up our circumstances to the one who is I AM, the one who is the same yesterday, today, and forever. It is a wise woman who builds the house of her life on the Rock of Christ. In Matthew 7:24 Jesus says that when we put His words into practice we are building on a rock. No matter what comes we will not be moved. Shiphrah and Puah stepped up on the rock, the steady foundation of their faith, and made a decision not based out of fear but based on trust in a God who determined their actions, who empowered them to make the right choice. And in this boldness to decide to let the children they delivered live, they were taking the power of death out of the hands of Pharaoh. Oh sure, he could have still called for their executions. Their decision could have still cost them their lives. We know that later Pharaoh still carried out his plan for a season, but not through them. For them the smile and pleasure of God was worth way more than the consequences from Egypt.

Because of this, the Lord blessed them. The Bible says that He gave them families of their own. We don't know the background of these two women, of how young or old they were, if they were single or if they were married and trying to conceive children themselves. Regardless of their stories, the Lord wrote a beautiful one for them and for us to follow. They sowed seeds of life by refusing to allow death to come by their hands and therefore reaped a harvest of life in their lives. Not only does your positioning on the Rock in the midst of tough decisions affect how you see the problem, but it affects how widespread the solution is. The solution for them was life, and it spilled over not only into the lives of the families they served but into their own families as well.

# PRESS IN

1. What was or could have been Shiphrah and Puah's strengths?

2. What was or could have been their weaknesses?

3. What is the biggest thing they needed to grasp during this time of beginnings?

4. What is the Holy Spirit saying to you about being His through the story of the midwives?

# 5

# Miriam

>>→

Numbers 12:1–6

## PROFILE

It is my last day here. Never in my life would I have pictured myself in this place. The past few days of my stay many pictures and images have gone through my mind, the emotions of those moments as potent as if they had happened much more recently than what seems like a lifetime ago. Never again do I want to see my body as it was during this time, rotting away, diseased and crippled with the leprosy I brought upon myself. But I know my time is over because I am now healed. My emotions swell as I look down at what has been restored. My hands...my hands are those of a slave, worn and weathered by the work they were forced to do. My feet...they are rough and callused, they have walked years in desert places; my voice, oh my voice...what had brought such rescue, such joy, also has revealed such pain and bitterness. Some could say it was inevitable. Isn't that one of the meanings of my name? Bitterness. I never intentionally embraced it; it was given out of the sorrow of our circumstances in Egypt. A picture of the brutality that I was born into. But now I know that bitterness consumed me, set fuel to my thoughts, justified my feelings, and set me on a course that I wish I never traveled.

Yet He is here. And every regret has faded away in the midst of His presence, for He is here and I am reminded that I do have worth. He is here, breaking every chain of shame, restoring my heart as He's healed my body. And within this tent, I don't know if I dwell alone or not. I may be left here in the desert, and that is still better than I deserve. But it matters because I have tasted the fruit of friendship, the tangibility of His presence. My brother saw Him on the mountain and I feel Him in this tent. His glory overflows and I am undone. It's as if He has pulled me out of the Nile, my own self I thrust into rivers of destruction because of offense and jealousy. Yet He draws me and reminds me that I am a rescuer even as He rescues me from myself. I am one who looks after the wellbeing of deliverers, not one who tears them down. I am one who leads the women in shouts of joy and praise, not in bellows of gossip and rage. I am a prophetess, speaking words of life, not death. And mostly He tells me, within and without, in a way only my heart can comprehend, that I indeed am His. And no sought-after position can confirm that more. We truly all are unworthy, yet He remembers us and knows us by name. He knows me by name. And yes I know, I believe that this knowing is enough for me.

I breathe out and every last wisp of fear is removed. It is time. I will leave this place that I have dwelled in for seven days. The time of my cleansing is finished, yet His command was more complete than I could comprehend. I open the flap, shielding my eyes from the foreign sun, love solidifying my step, love casting out the fear, love determining that as I wander this desert potentially without my people, my joy will remain.

My eyes adjust to the light and as they focus...oh, my heart. I must be seeing a vision. Surely this is not right. Instead of empty wilderness before me there is a sea of people, belongings ready, standing at attention. They have not left me behind. I feel the kiss of heaven; the gift I had forfeited but have had returned. And in the front, walking, no, now running before me are my brothers. I almost laugh as those old men race toward me, the limits of age gone for the moment, excitement quickening their steps. And before I can even catch my breath I am engulfed in their strong arms. I do not know if the tears belong to them or me, but a river flows between us. Forgiveness is in our midst and the one I followed along a riverbank, the one I watched return boldly to fight for his people, the one who has led and performed miracles, the one who is a friend to God kisses me on the forehead and tells me to come. I am remembered, I am not forgotten, I am restored.

# PONDER

I've suffered from the same. We all do at times in our lives. The same need to be a part of something, to be involved, to matter in the areas we deem important. Before we know it our identities become wrapped up in what we do instead of in who we are. So in order to continue to feel the worth we crave and receive the affirmation we think we need, we continue down our path to bitterness and jealousy. We start to compare ourselves to others instead of to Him who made us.

When Miriam chose to follow her brother along the Nile as a young woman or maybe as a child, she didn't do so for the accolades, pats on the back, or congrats. She didn't do so as merely a role to play or a job that she *had* to do. She was hidden, crouching within the reeds, praying and pleading that her brother would remain safe. She was a sister, aching for a brother released to a river and to the hands of God—a God they supposedly hadn't heard from in hundreds of years. She saw her mother weeping, the depth of her father's grief, and was compelled to move out of the overflow of her nurturing heart. And when that basket was delivered from the waters and she saw her brother in the hands of her people's enemy, her humility and boldness empowered her to speak words of wisdom and creativity, even at such a young age. She determined to solve the problems that were plaguing her personal environment, at least for a little while.

After years of watching from a distance, of releasing her brother not just into the arms of a princess but years later into the grasp of the wilderness, her heart probably could not contain her joy when her baby brother returned. It simmered and bubbled throughout the months of plagues and miracles, doubts and answers until it overflowed out of every pore of her being. She rejoiced openly, dancing out her deliverance, clearing a path for others to do the same.

She was seeing the fruition of her act as a child, and there was such security found in her place as sister of Moses, prophetess of Israel. What she had done out of inspiration and need firmly planted her in a place of influence. We don't know where and we can only ask the Holy Spirit for how, but her source of affirmation, her drive to act, shifted from God-inspired and heart-centered to image-driven and title-focused. We find her in Numbers 12, along with her other brother, Aaron, opposing her baby brother, Moses. She had come a long way from protecting her brother to now standing against him. All because of who he married—and thinking she should have been given a better position in the eyes of the Israelites and in her own. Miriam wanted to be treated with more honor. She traded her primary, eternal significance as a child of God for the temporary lure of works-based leadership.

We fool ourselves into thinking our worth comes from man. These are the norms that plague our existence, yet this was not the intention from the beginning. The scary part is that for many of us it happens unintentionally. If we are not continually aligning ourselves with the Holy Spirit we will find ourselves unaligned with His heart toward us. I was a junior high pastor for eight years, teaching students on a weekly basis, leading small groups, and mentoring girls. I moved out of the passion and overflow of my heart to impact this age group and lead them to Jesus. But I began to realize the extent of my sway when I could not read the Bible for myself anymore; I could not feed me. I would read the Word of God but my mind would immediately catalogue it into a message, a topic of discussion, or an illustration, and it wasn't getting to the depth of me. I wasn't allowing His words to change *me*.

My every move was shackled by the fear of man, and instead of walking in freedom as a daughter I was stumbling along on eggshells and within boxes of my own making. Bitterness began to leak through my being because I thought I wasn't being noticed or recognized. I discounted my significance before God and waited for others to give it to me as if I was a drug addict. It wasn't until I felt the call to release that role and then sat in the seclusion of maternity leave that I was able to quiet myself down enough to hear the whisper of my Father. His main question to me was this: "Are you satisfied in Me?" I had to take a hard look at myself, and I answered as honestly as I could. "No" was my response. I wasn't satisfied in Christ, because instead of craving His approval I was seeking the approval of others. I was using it as my oxygen and letting people shift the atmosphere inside of me. It was shifting me.

When God called me to lay down my role as junior high pastor it wasn't just about stepping into a new role or even because there was a baby on the way. I believe He wanted to get me in a place where I would not be distracted and would hear from Him more clearly. In those weeks God began to deliver me from the fear of man, and still today I make the choice daily to not be swayed. Many days it is a fight to remain with eyes focused on Him. Because I know that when I am satisfied in Christ there is no position or job title that can complete me or compete with His approval. You must know that when you allow Jesus to be the center of what you do, to be validated fully by Him, no flattery or criticism can shift your core. You can operate in an immovable confidence because your center is centered on Him. He is the solid rock who will not shift despite what others say or do or don't say or do.

In the same way Miriam's very punishment, God's consequence for her, showed how much she really did matter. It took seven days—days of completion for her to remember again. I believe that Miriam's time outside of the camp, to cleanse her from her leprosy, was also a way to cleanse her heart. God must have reminded her of who she was and what He had called her to do. It didn't matter what position she thought she should have. It only mattered how she was positioned in Him. This is true freedom, and there is no one better to be known by than to be known by the Lord. Not only do I believe that tent was the tent of her deliverance, but the Lord capped it off by having the camp not move until she was fully cleansed. She walked out of that tent to a sea of people waiting for her. Numbers 12:15 says "And the people did not move from that place until she was brought in again" (ERV). What a beautiful picture of the mercy of God. Just like she patiently waited by the side of a river for her brother to be rescued, God allowed for the people of Israel to stay and wait patiently as He worked on rescuing her soul. He was giving Miriam what she didn't deserve and reminding her of her worth, unattached to any title, position, or role.

# PRESS IN

1. What was or could have been Miriam's strength?

2. What was or could have been her weakness?

3. What is the biggest thing she needed to grasp during this time of beginnings?

4. What is the Holy Spirit saying to you about being His through Miriam's story?

# Prayer

>>→

*Lord, I thank You for the stories of these women during a time of beginnings. These women helped lay a foundation for our faith even during times of great temptation, trial, and testing. We go beyond just learning from their choices into looking at our own selves in the mirror. Let the words that You have inspired about them cut into our very souls. May we remove the lies and remember that we belong to You above all else and therefore can be empowered to make the choices that glorify Your name. We are not defined by our mistakes if we allow them to be covered in Your blood, so please forgive us; we repent of anything that doesn't line up with Your heart and Your ways. We want to become more like You. We want to be the daughters You have intended us to be so that we can walk with full confidence in the plans that You have for us. May Your affirmation and truth be the foundation of our lives. We love You. Jesus; thank You for dying on the cross and rising from death to make true love a reality for us. Amen.*

# PART 2

>>→

# His in the Promise

*She is His.*
*And because of that she is brave, beautiful,*
*bold, and strong.*
*She laughs at the days to come knowing that her*
*work comes from her rest.*
*Leaning on the one who knows her best, she sets her*
*rhythm to the cadence of His heart.*
*Moves where He moves, goes where He goes, breathes*
*in time with Him.*
*For in Him is the fullness of her joy and the source of*
*her satisfaction.*
*She rests easy, she is covered, her strength dwelling in*
*what she yields to Him.*
*A force to be reckoned with because she is only His.*

# 6

# Daughters of Zelophehad

>>→

Numbers 27:1–11; 36:1–12

## PROFILE

Laying our father to rest was one of the hardest things we'd ever done. Seeing our hero brought low by doubt and unbelief was difficult, but we never knew our worst fears would be realized. He *had* to die. He'd been swayed by the crowd, given in to fear, and voiced the wrong thing. Those were still his choices and so would be his consequences to bear. But now that our grief is over there is another obstacle looming before us. Would his inheritance, *our* inheritance be buried with him? Just because the Lord chose not to give him sons? Surely He was more merciful than that. Surely he will see our plight and come to our rescue. We now have no other Father but Him.

Zelophehad, our earthly father, has been dead only a few days, yet we know we have to move. If we remain silent and succumb to the weight of tradition his name could be lost forever and maybe our voice with him too. We are afraid; we don't know what the response will be, we don't know if even stepping out could mean our disgrace or death. But something compels us forward. No, as we smile to each other amidst our fears, *Someone* beckons us to come. We've heard mostly of His power, seen the daily provision of water and manna, and our hearts remind us that though our father is gone, buried in the desert for his own sin…there is another one who must know our names.

We awake early and dress in our finest. Not to impress but to honor. We want to bring our best. Our mourning attire is laid down and we take up joy instead, letting it clothe our hearts and our minds. We are not orphans; we and all of Israel belong to someone greater than any earthly father. And in that confidence we will make our request known. The assembly has gathered, and as we continue to make our way forward we ignore the stares, the murmurs and whispers. We will not let our fear grow; we will not be distracted from our task. We are sisters banded together for one purpose and our common goal, our common love makes us strong. When we are almost there we do something we haven't done since we were children. We clasp hands, some cold, some moist with sweat, but all squeezing so tight, holding on, united. We are sisters and we go to speak to our Father.

As the oldest, I step out, my younger sisters behind me like a rear guard. I lower my hand and gaze in honor of the one who stands before me. God's instrument of deliverance for our people, the one used to part seas, to bring the Egyptian nation to her knees. I lift my eyes, and when I meet his gaze his eyes light up in question, but not rejection. The urgency of my request keeps me from running away or, really, into his arms. He who walked in the palace and desert, who was a prince and shepherd, he who is called a friend of God. What wonders he must know.

When he allows, I make our plea known. We have practiced the words many times, but even so they are sincere and they come from a true desire to honor our father. When I finish Moses nods and leaves to hear from the Lord, I assume. His desire to seek an answer rather than dismiss us with a quick no bolsters our courage. My sisters surround me as we wait, minutes seeming to be days as we consider every scenario, every possibility. When Moses returns there is firmness and authority in his expression as he turns to address the crowd, but as he looks at us—oh, how we miss our father—there is tenderness in his gaze and a smile on his face. Our request has been heard and accepted. We are not left uncovered.

# PONDER

Apologies can be a balm to a wounded soul, the words needed to set things right. When they arise from hearts of sincerity they can be used as an avenue of healing to those who are broken, a way to bridge the gap between two separate hearts. I believe that saying sorry is one of the quickest ways to the path of humility. It bypasses all the scenic routes and dives right into the heart of the issue. It displays a level of transparency and vulnerability that might not have otherwise been seen. But this is not what I want to focus on here.

"Sorry," "I apologize," or "That was my fault" are major parts of my vocabulary. It is probably because my imperfections far out-weigh my strengths, and I have the need to make things right more than others. At times it is because I want to see peace manifest in certain circumstances, and offering myself on an altar can be a way to open up dialogue to create a space for healing. I would like to say this is my motive most of the time. But unfortunately, these words can often come from a place of insecurity and fear of man. I have to assume that I am not the only one who struggles with this. In her book, *The Best Yes*, Lysa TerKeurst calls it the "disease to please."[2] That phrase in itself gets to the heart of me like an arrow and always seems to find areas that I have not yet surrendered to the Lord.

You may have it more together and therefore have motives that are aligned with a heart of pure humility and love. But many of you may be like me, struggling to gain approval from people and willing to do whatever it takes to get it. I don't care if you are allowing yourself to be played with by every guy who passes through your life or if you are a stay-at-home mom with Pinterest envy or even a missionary on a foreign field longing for home. If we are not rooted in our identity as daughters of God, we will seek approval and affirmation from those who were never meant to give it to us. Therefore, we will do our best to be all that we can be for those people and/or situations, and when we are not...we will apologize, say we are sorry, and claim that it is our fault for what we believe to be our failures.

I'm not saying that there isn't a place for true repentance when we mess up. Of course there is. Of course there is a turning from our sin, that which separates us from our Father, and turning to Him. But when we are not rooted in His love we begin to claim things that we were never meant to carry. Burden our shoulders with tasks and responsibilities that were never ours to bear. We even take the blame for mistakes that were not ours or problems that were never meant to be solved by us. Why? Because somehow we believe if we get it right we can gain approval. And if we get it wrong, our sorry and apologies become masks for the pain of failure, the pain of once again not being good enough. So we back away and cower in our self-inflicted shame, running from the very one who restores. We stay away until we see another way that we can prove ourselves, another standard to attain to.

This was not so for the daughters of Zelophehad. In a time of strict law and tradition, they found boldness to move forward from the words of God into His whispers and His ways. They knew that they had an earthly father who was no longer with them, perhaps dying an untimely death in the desert with the rest of unbelieving Israel. But they would not claim his sin as their own. They did not allow his past mistakes to place a pallor on their present situation.

And it was very bleak for them looking in from the outside. They had no brothers to inherit their father's wealth and continue taking care of them. There were no men currently in line for them to marry and therefore be provided for. The world of the Old Testament was not the easiest time for women on their own. They just had the five of them—sisters, a beautiful *grace*-full number. They decided that they would not stay where they were. They wouldn't allow their father's name and all that was his to die in the dust with him.

For you to move forward toward the one you belong to you must break off the chains of your past and your family's history. Their sin does not have to be your own. But if you continue in agreement with it, claiming it as some sort of twisted inheritance, you will not have the freedom to move forward the way God has called you to. We all have our histories, and some of them are so intense it seems as if we take one step forward and are pulled three steps back. But through Jesus who accomplished your complete deliverance all on the cross, you have the authority, dear daughter, to break those generational curses…when you understand that you are His. You belong to *Him*. You can break off what never should have belonged to you anyway and claim the righteous inheritance that is yours for the taking. Why? Because beyond any earthly family, you have one who is more of a Father to you than anyone you could know. You are a daughter. And when daughters know who they are, they are not concerned with anyone else around them. You don't have to prod them to approach their daddy. They run with arms wide open, leaping, dancing, kissing, hugging, talking, gabbing, crying, smiling all over their Father. It's the type of confidence that Hebrews 4:16 speaks of, confidence to approach the throne room boldly in your time of need. And our times of greatest need are not when we want Daddy's credit card or permission for something we want to do. It's when we need to grab hold of what has already been purchased for us, the inheritance that is already ours, so that we can step out in the promises that He has laid before us. Despite the circumstances, despite the obstacles, despite what fear wants to dictate to us.

The daughters of Zelophehad had an inheritance to claim. And they would not even let laws and traditions stop them from stepping out boldly. They stepped out together, strength in their number, not sorry for being created as women, not sorry for falling short of societal inheritance standards, not taking the blame for the sins their father or anyone else had committed. They stepped forward in the presence of the people, Moses, and God and petitioned for their inheritance. They laid claim on the nature of God that they had a revelation of—that He was a good father and would surely not leave them bereft and uncovered.

The beautiful thing about this boldness was that not only did they receive what they asked for, but also a new law was put into place that would affect other women in similar situations in the future. When we settle into our fears and allow a performance mentality to rule us we miss the opportunities to make waves in the Kingdom because instead of being focused on the heart of our Father we are focused on the pleasure of other ones who can never fulfill us. These are the ones who do not have the power of life and death over us, but we give it to them every day. The "them" for you may be established traditions or norms, friends, family, society, or maybe it's the one looking back at you in the mirror. Maybe you are the one putting expectations on yourself that God never meant for you to carry. He said His burden is easy and His yoke is light, not because our lives as believers are cakewalks, but because when the yoke fits the way He intended it to there are no hindrances. When we are yoked to Him there is no stopping what He wants to accomplish. Stop apologizing for something or rather *someone* you were never meant to be, repent sincerely for fearing man over God, and step boldly to the Father who loves you more than anything.

# PRESS IN

1. What was or could have been the daughters' strength?

2. What was or could have been their weakness?

3. What is the biggest thing the daughters needed to grasp during this time of promise?

4. What is the Holy Spirit saying to you about being His through the story of the daughters of Zelophehad?

# 7

# Rahab

>>→

## PROFILE

The time is drawing near. I can feel it in my bones. My grandmother used to say the same thing when the atmosphere changed or the seasons shifted. I am not anywhere near her age but I might as well be. It feels like I've lived a thousand lifetimes, all through the eyes of men who I thought loved me. I learned to sense their every mood, every longing until I choked on disgust of myself. Maybe it would have been better if I loved them too. But I had left that a long time ago. Love had left me too vulnerable, too open to getting hurt. Until…Him. Until the stories that traveled across cities and through messengers until they found their way to me. But what I was sensing did not have to do with men. Something was unsettled in the air; there was a rumbling in my heart that made my fingers tremble. They were coming.

I quickly assess my items and make sure I haven't missed anything that is important to take with me. Most everything I have is tainted with my sin; they are not worthy to go with me on what-ever journey lies ahead. After double-checking, I leave my home and walk down the steps that will lead me away from my house within the walls and into the more central part of the city. I warned them. My family knows I will come at some point but I still pray fever-ishly, in the best way I know how, to the God who is headed toward our city.

We had *all* heard the stories. And while some dismissed them as rumors and most cowered in fear, I grabbed on to the hope that was being revealed. There was someone out there more powerful than the bloodthirsty gods of my people. I had seen too much, too many babies sacrificed at the altars of convenience. Their lives were given to ensure prosperity or profit or pleasure for the giver. People cheated out of their homes and inheritances. Lust-filled men and women having their way with the innocent to satisfy their own selfish needs. Isn't that where I started? An object of abuse left to salvage my life the best way I knew. Continuing to perform as I'd been performed upon to at least make a living from my shame. I turned love into a weapon that would be used to break the hearts of men and harden mine in the process. Until Him.

I pause before I reach my family's dwelling. Until Him. My hand against my chest cannot calm the emotion rising within me. Some laughed at the stories, but they were words that began to chip away at my heart, break the walls I had put in place to protect myself. If this God could split the Red Sea and in moments wipe out an army in its waters, surely He could cleanse the stain of my shame. Surely He could erase what my mind could not. And when I saw those two men, so unlike our own, I knew. But instead of fear at our fate, desperation took over me. I wanted to hear more and to escape. I went against the wishes of those who sought them out, and I hid them. I would not let the hope that came to my door be executed at the hands of my fearful people. And in exchange they promised me my life—my life! It wasn't just about remaining for a longer period of time in this physical body. It was about the new life I could embark on; the new journey I could start. A journey away from all the things that I wanted to forget. And I could only pray that I would be welcomed by the people who were on the way to destroy everything that I'd ever known.

I knock hurriedly on my family's door. As a precaution I look around me to make sure no one is watching. I am still under suspicion after the incident with the spies, especially because they were never found. However, I am untouched because for the most part everyone assumes that the spies merely came to me to fulfill their pleasurable desires and to find a place to stay. Because what more could a prostitute be known for? To my people she could never be known as someone more. I was just an object of lustful attention. But not to those spies. Never had I met such honorable men. I didn't even cower at their wary eyes and initial judgment of me. I had always been a piece of meat to be surveyed and devoured and I relished the freedom that their brief presence brought. Even with the risk I tried to warn as many as I could. I tried to open up the possibilities of a powerful God, but instead of embracing what I was saying my people shunned me even more and stood fast in their fear. Thankfully my family, oh my family, decided to follow me and take a chance on what I shared with them. I didn't tell them too much about my encounter with the spies. I didn't want them to have to carry the burden of knowledge just in case the officials of Jericho asked them any questions.

I knock again. When the door opens my mother stands before me, knowing in her eyes. I can't say anything; the stress of the past few weeks tumbles out of me as she draws me into a tight embrace. We have had our difficulties, our moments of familial crisis. She didn't believe me years ago when I said that her own brother had been the one to take my innocence, but in this embrace I feel her strength, I feel the support, and I feel her regret. Many years between mother and daughter have been lost. But in this risk that means more to me than anything else, she believes me. She did not doubt, and even now she is ready. She releases me from her grasp and turns to the rest of the family standing or sitting in fear around the room. She nods at each one and looks back at me, resignation setting her features. "It is time."

By the time we return to my home in the wall I can already feel the march of an army, the questions and calls of the people in the city. They are in fear, but I am in peace. The God I do not fully know but who somehow must fully love me has provided a way for me not just to be rescued but, I hope, to know Him. I place in my window the symbol of my salvation and pull my family close as we wait. Today is the day of our deliverance.

# PONDER

The beauty of a choice. The choice to incline one's ear to rumor, to mystery. Not to the poison and intrigue of gossip but the whispers of the eternal that reverberate off our environments, beckoning us to come a little closer, to dig a little deeper. They are the leadings that cause us to pause in the midst of the norm of our lives and ask, "Could this be true? Is there more than this? Is there more to me?" It's realizing that the longings that continually permeate our hearts actually have a source and satisfaction and it may be beyond all that we've ever known. It is the choice to move past what's been constant and to believe that there is something waiting for us to discover. This is the choice that Rahab made, and it changed her life forever.

The story of Rahab is one of the most beautiful in the Bible. There is such contrast within the story—the end of the old and the beginning of the new, the dawn of promise and the threat of destruction, the darkness of circumstance and the decision to be brave. In the middle of much turmoil Rahab stands out as a poignant pillar of what it means to have faith. Her choice wasn't made in the midst of daylight. She wasn't surrounded by those who were eager to go the same direction she was going in. But despite any external pressures or even lack of concern Rahab decided that she was going to trust in the God she was hearing stories about versus the gods of her people that she had been raised with. As she was wrestling with what she would believe there were a people, a covenant people, making preparations to enter her land.

On the other side of the Jordan, the people of Israel were camped, ready for what lay before them. The men recovered from the process of their recommitment to God, awaiting instructions from their commander about what move to make. Before this Joshua had sent two spies to scout out the land of Jericho, the city that stood at the door of their promise. The Israelites were strong and confident; those who had come into agreement with negativity and doubt were no longer among the populace. Those who remained had a fresh vision of God's purposes, and under the leadership of Joshua and the inspiration of Caleb they were ready to possess their inheritance, their promised land. There should have been no hindrance to their victory. There was no reason for them to entertain a thought of defeat...yet Joshua sent spies. Two men who were tasked with assessing the strength of the city, but instead were impacted by the strong faith of a prostitute.

Sometimes I don't think we realize the significance of our response when various situations arise in our lives. Like Eve forgetting the importance of the eternal, we many times put more hope in what we see before us than the reality of the unseen. Even as I type these words I have to put a mirror in front of my own self as well. Whether on the mountaintop or valley low, there are always distractions vying for our attention, trying to drain our resolve, pull us from our focus. We wade through the traditions of our past or even the experiences of our present, trying to move forward in our relationship with Christ or just to move at all. Maybe some of our stories are like that of Rahab. We find ourselves in beds that we have made or that we were forced into. Many times we let our mistakes disqualify us from our God-dream, but it's even in those instances that God wants to bring restoration and hope. Or maybe we willingly choose the wrong direction because we think that it doesn't matter what we do anymore.

All the while our God is moving, causing miracles, setting things in order, bringing things to fullness, impacting with His Presence. Will we be ones who settle for our normal existence, or will we choose to believe that there is truly more? That there is someone, not something, whom we can have relationship with. Imagine the boldness of Rahab. While those around her shuddered in fear or put up walls of resistance, she opened her heart fully to the God of Israel she heard stories about. As her people continued to sacrifice to the demonic idols, she began to position herself to give over her life to the one true God. I don't know how this exactly played out in the days, weeks, months, or even years before the spies arrived at her city. Only heaven will tell us the extent of her possible prayers or supplication to this foreign God who had split the seas and pronounced judgment on the nation of Egypt. But we know that somehow, through the stories that had made their way to Jericho, God was wooing these people. He was making sure that His Word was known even to them. How merciful our God is—even when we don't realize it, there is a wooing, a drawing, a leading to His heart. It is His will that none should perish...not them, not you.

Even though the entire city was aware of what had taken place, only Rahab responded. I don't believe that the spies were sent to just check out the land. Maybe for them that was the only reason. I believe there was a divine plan taking place, a heavenly response to an earthly request. Within the darkness of Jericho there was a heart beating for more, to know more, to see more, to be more, and He heard. So for a Father whose heart was bent toward His daughter, it would be nothing to cause a nation to pause, to allow two men to be sent on an errand, all for the purpose of rescuing her. Think about it. Victory was already in hand; there was much assurance in the ability of God to deliver. So much so that in the next battle, when there was actual defeat, the people of Israel threw themselves down before the Lord, crying out to ask what had gone wrong. For them, winning the battle was the only option. And for the Lord, moving heaven and earth to free His daughter was a given. Even the angel of the Lord that met Joshua at the wall made sure to include Rahab in his instructions.

Rahab was His even when within her society she seemed to belong to everyone else. With her house being located within the wall of Jericho, who knows how many people crossed her path, who knows how many men she shared her bed with. The Bible doesn't give us her full history; we are not told why her life had come to the point of prostitution. The Word just gives us her occupation when the spies came in contact with her and how beautifully she responded when she was presented with the very ones she was sup-posed to fear. She chose to protect the messengers who were sent, shield them from her people, and in boldness asked for her life and the life of her family. Salvation had come to her, and she made sure it would come to her household as well. A cord hung form her win-dow represented the submission of her heart to the blood of the lamb, like the blood that was placed on the doorposts of the people of Israel in Egypt, like the blood that would one day flow from her messianic descendant. Rahab was not just some insignificant player in history. She was a woman who decided to cast off restraint and throw everything she had into belonging to this covenant people, this one true God.

Her character did not just stop when she was rescued. We know from the Word that not only did she marry one of the Israelites but she gave birth to a man name Boaz. We know that Boaz acted in bold righteousness and character himself when he reached out in kindness to the widow Ruth and helped redeem the family of Naomi. How well his mother Rahab must have taught him! In Ruth's story we can see how highly he must have valued the insight and perspective of his foreign-born mother. And from the line of Boaz and Ruth we know came not only Israel's anointed worshiping warrior king but the Messiah who would save all people.

Wow! We cannot read this story and fail to see how much it applies to us. Oh sister, you are significant, your voice, your cries, your words, your prayers mean something. No matter what the enemy tries to throw your way, no matter what circumstance has tried to weigh you down, your response matters. Because there is a King in heaven who is attentive to you and will do everything in His power to rescue you. I don't know what it will look like exactly or the timing of His intervention. But for you, darling, He will send messengers; for you He will pause an army; for you, baby girl, He will break down walls and pull you into the grand destiny He has for you. Don't let the shame of your experiences keep you from speaking; don't allow the mistakes you've made keep you from stepping out boldly. He says we can come to Him boldly—boldly! Not in pride or in slight dismissal of our sin, but in humility, in repentance, in whatever response is warranted, being fully confident that our God is ready to wrap us in His arms and call us His own.

We are the ones blessed to see the lives and actions of these people from our modern perspective, but most of them had no idea what God would do through their lives. And that's where faith comes in, trusting that you matter, that you are not forgotten. You can be confident that when you seek Him you will find Him because He has already found you. Wherever you are, wherever you are hiding. Even when people reject you, God does not reject you and heaven knows your name.

# PRESS IN

1. What was or could have been Rahab's strength?

2. What was or could have been her weakness?

3. What is the biggest thing she needed to grasp during this time of promise?

4. What is the Holy Spirit saying to you about being His through Rahab's story?

# 8

# Jael

>>→

JUDGES 4:17–22; 5:6,24–27

## PROFILE

My husband comes into the tent in a rush, his chest heaving with labored breaths as if he's been running. His brown face pours with stress and I see the fear in his face. "What is it, husband?" I go to him taking his large hand in both of mine, willing him to calm down. "Is it as the reports said?" He can barely nod; his breaths are so heavy. "Yes, they are true. Barak has routed Sisera and his chariots, but that is not what causes me panic, my love" He sits down, no longer able to stand. "My scouts tell me that Sisera is coming in this direction!" "How far off is he?" I can feel the fear rising in my chest. My husband's family has always been on cordial terms with King Jabin. Heber has done what he can to maintain peace with those around him. But Jabin's commander Sisera is a man without conscience and ruthless. I had only seen him once and trembled in fear then. And now he is headed this way.

I swallow my trembling the best I can. "How long, husband?" He looks at me with wild eyes. I have never seen that expression on his face. "In a matter of moments!" He jumps up suddenly. "He is still on his chariot; it won't be long now. He will come here to hide and then bring the wrath of Barak upon us!" My husband begins to run around the tent, grasping items, searching for our valuables. In that moment my world stops. I see my husband moving as if in slow motion, terror a train behind him. I see my life and all the moments I allowed fear to take over, had been silent when I should have spoken up, when I ran away instead of standing firm. Now potential calamity is about to cross our threshold, and strange peace takes hold of me. I remember the words we heard of the God of the Hebrews, strong and mighty, yet friend of our distant relative Moses. I will not fear death this day but I will fear Him. Even as these thoughts enter, a plan begins to weave its way into my consciousness. And I smile.

"What are you doing?!" Time continues and my husband's voice is almost a shriek. "Did you not hear me woman? We need to leave now. Gather the children, get your belongings. War is upon our house!" My mouth moves into a thin line. "And we will be the victors." Instead of gathering my things I begin to tidy up. I take out the goat's milk, bread, and cheese I was saving for the midday meal. "Be at peace, husband." I turn to him before he can say anything else. "Go and stand with the children, make sure our herds and flocks are in order. Calm the servants and shepherds. But I will not leave here." Shock engulfs my husband's face. But something in my resolve makes him not question me anymore. He simply nods in shock and runs out to do as I ask.

Later I stand at the doorway of my tent and shield my eyes against the sun. As I move my gaze across the horizon a small dust cloud draws my attention. As the seconds pass it grows bigger until I see there are horses and a chariot attached to it. It is Sisera. As he drives closer I walk toward him. Seeing that it is just me, the small-statured, defenseless wife of Heber, he dismounts and almost stumbles my way. I see his weariness and any other semblance of my fear disappears in the wind. "My lord, come into my tent. Do not be afraid, you can come hide here." His usually hard exterior has fallen with his defeat and exhaustion. He comes to me without a struggle, as if a child being led by his mother. He collapses onto my bedding; I cover him with my blanket. Water he asks for, so I give him milk. Bread and cheese I also serve until his eyes are heavy with sleep and satiation. I wait for his snoring and then move toward a tent peg I have hidden in the corner. These arms are strengthened by the constant task of moving and setting tents. My work is done quickly.

Only a few hours pass. My husband and I sit outside waiting. The children are with the servants, not allowed to come in. My ordeal has left me a bit weak so I lean against a pillow, eyes closed, until Heber leans into me. "They are here." He helps me up, awe still in his eyes, and walks with me toward the arriving party. By his bearing and the number of men who flank him I know this is Barak, leader of the Israeli army. And out from behind him comes one who I have heard rumors of. Deborah, the Judge. She looks older than I, whether from age or wisdom. Her hair is wind-whipped and out of place, her skin glowing with the sweat of her victory. Her eyes intense and knowing. She is beautiful. This is what it must look like for someone to be a friend of the God of Israel.

"I know who you are in pursuit of, my lord," I say before they can even speak. "Come and see." Barak looks at me strangely but dismounts quickly, the weapons at his side still bloody. Deborah has a smile on her face as if she already knows. I draw back the opening of the tent and show them the man they are searching for. He looks as if he is asleep but on closer inspection they see what my hands have done. Sisera lies dead with a tent peg through his temple. A victorious shout comes from the men and laughter from Deborah. She looks at Barak with her eyes alight with joy. "Did I not tell you that he would be delivered into the hands of a woman?" She turns to me and embraces me with a motherly hug. "Today you are most blessed of women! You have defeated the enemy that came to your door and set free the captives of Israel!"

# PONDER

I love that in the Bible there seem to be many stories of unsuspecting women who make a huge difference. Or at least for us if we were to meet them face to face we would never suspect the potential that is beneath their surface. We just looked briefly at the life of Rahab and her extraordinary leap of faith in harboring the Hebrew spies and choosing the God of Israel over her own traditional gods and ways. In this story we have two women who affected a nation. One a known leader and judge and another a home maker. But yet they worked so beautifully together to bring victory to Israel without even knowing the other initially. I think about how many times women say they don't like being around other women because of drama, comparison, insecurities, or whatever reasons we give for not participating in sisterhood. But not only are the ones in our spheres of influence our sisters but so also are the ones we have never met. Our relationship with Jesus can have enormous influence in ways we don't even recognize.

The most amazing part of this is that it doesn't matter what our current role is. Deborah was a highly respected judge in Israel. She was married and possibly a mother even though the Bible doesn't tell us of biological children. It does say, "She rose up, a mother in Israel." Even if she didn't have children she had given birth to, she operated in a nurturing and empowering role. She gave out judgments to the people and led with the words of the Lord as her authority. A mother who is operating the way that God intended for her to will not only give wisdom to those around her but will seek to empower the men and women in her life. She gave a directive to Barak from the Lord, encouraging him to go out and fight because the Lord would give him victory. When he hesitated and asked if she would accompany him, she agreed but also said because of his pause the credit would go to a woman.

At first glance it may seem like she was referring to herself, and maybe indeed she was. But it's interesting that she didn't say she herself would get the credit specifically, but that a woman would. It's as if prophetically she was opening the door and allowing herself to represent all the women in her nation. Maybe God gave her a glimpse into the future and showed her exactly how things would go down. Or maybe she was just a woman like you and me, longing for her sisters to rise up and be who God called them to be. Women who would take their place in the battle and fight the way the Lord had equipped them to. For Deborah, she used the words and revelation given. For Jael, well, she used something that was solely designed to hold her tent down.

Jael. A seemingly insignificant housewife among the many wives, mothers, and sisters of ancient Israel and the surrounding area. Her day was probably filled with the normal chores and routine of child care, shepherding, farming, cooking, cleaning. She too was married, but she did not sit under a palm like Deborah did and give out judgments to the public. Her words were confined to what she shared with her husband or children or servants. Yet she was not insignificant, was she? How many times do we get caught up in our roles and underestimate the significance of what season of life we are in? This is not an argument between whether women should stay at home or be a part of the workplace. We may have our ideals and our thoughts and our traditions, but really we are meant to be who God has called us to be. We are meant to be led by the Spirit and to submit to His guiding.

For those of us unmarried, we are meant to be in submission to our father or the authorities in our lives who give us wisdom. For those of us married, we are meant to be in submission to our husbands and their authority. It's not about being less than, but choosing to operate in a place of release and freedom that only God can ordain. It is the position of Christ and the church, a beautiful partnership intended to bring positive impact. Neither Deborah nor Jael were in the wrong places or the specifically right places. They were exactly where they were supposed to be. Deborah was in the place to hear the word of the Lord and share it with Barak and speak prophetically about the role of women in the battle. Jael was meant to be about the business of her household, conveniently on the route that Sisera would take, conveniently among the family that had friendly relations with his king. And therefore she was right where she needed to be to take action against the enemy.

Think about it, sister. The battle she fought in her home put the seal on the battle that was already being won around her. Sure, maybe she could have left him alone and Barak would have still defeated him. But she would not leave room to question or to chance. Jael recognized that there was something bigger that they were fighting for, and a friendly, familiar enemy was still her enemy. She took action to make sure it would be done completely. When we are dealing with issues in our own personal lives, we may assume that it doesn't have anything to do with anything else. We may think that we are the only ones affected; therefore, we will be the only ones to see victory or defeat. Those issues may be so familiar to us that we think they don't really matter. But you must know that you *are* more significant than you realize and the battles you fight in the privacy of your own home can have ramifications in your family, your community, your world.

A man named Achan realized this when he took items that he was specifically told not to take into his home. Before the battle of Jericho several years before this story of Jael, the Lord told Joshua that the Israelites were to destroy everything completely and not take any plunder because these things were devoted to destruction. Destruction was attached to these items. The only ones who would be saved would be the household of Rahab because she came into agreement with the will and Kingdom of God. Yet somehow Achan did not think he was significant enough to be noticed, and he took some of the things that were desirable to his eye. Because of this, the next battle the Israelites fought was met with defeat. Achan's family was destroyed as a result of his greed, because he took into his home what was meant to be destroyed. We cannot fight the enemies outside of us if we are harboring enemies on the inside. You can't have victory over something you are in agreement with. You won't have authority over something that you have given your authority to. You can play a significant role whether for the good or otherwise.

Hear me, sister. Where are your tent pegs? What are the skills and gifts, the seemingly mundane activities that your hands have grown accustomed to? He could be asking you to use those things to wage war against all that assails you. What enemy that once had easy access to your house is the Lord asking you to destroy? Your future battles hinge on the ones you fight now; the victory of a generation is waiting to be sealed by how you respond. Maybe it's a lot of pressure for a housewife, maybe it's a lot of pressure for a single mom, maybe it's a lot of pressure for a woman who works outside of the home, maybe it's a lot of pressure for a daughter, but daughter—you have the backing of your Father. He has given you all that you need. You are His and you can do it victoriously through Jesus Christ who strengthens your hands.

# PRESS IN

1. What was or could have been Jael's strength?

2. What was or could have been her weakness?

3. What is the biggest thing she needed to grasp during this time of promise?

4. What is the Holy Spirit saying to you about being His through Jael's story?

# 9

# Ruth

>>→

## PROFILE

"Go." The words are full of release, and I know there is no turning back now. I don't know why I chose to agree with this plan, but I know she has never done anything to hurt me. Even in her darkest moments she has shown the light of her soul, depression and distress not dampening her fragile hope. Because instead of giving up she went home. And I came with her. Despite the loss in our lives, there was more I desired to gain. The one who I knew could never be taken from me because she hadn't allowed Him to be taken from her.

I will never forget that day. The grief of our departure had been palpable. Each step I took away from the city only gave me a clearer picture of the oppressive fog that covered it. Each time I looked back a new memory assaulted me. Some lighter ones—laughter with friends, the innocence of childhood. Some sweet ones—the first day

I saw Kilion in the marketplace, how handsome he was during those days. And the bitter—the image of Kilion's sunken-in face; oh how quickly the sickness had gone through his body. How terribly it had ravaged his strong physique. There were a few dark memories too—the worship of Chemosh and the horrific practices involved. I had shuddered then and I shudder now.

Despite almost several decades of my life spent in that city, I did not want to stay. I wanted to take a chance on love again. I wanted more than the physical; I needed the God my mother-in-law talked of. I needed to know that there was someone more real and more loving and more in control than the ones my people worshiped. We stopped about a mile outside of the city, all three of us already tired. The burdens we carried not just from the packs on our backs. It was then that our number decreased. Naomi was losing hope quickly, and she did not want her fate to be ours. She pleaded with my sister-in-law and I to leave, to go back to the city and start new lives for ourselves. Orpah was hesitant but then took the opportunity to leave. I had known her from childhood. Her beauty had remained and so would her prospects.

Orpah started to head back and then turned to me as if expecting me to follow. Naomi grasped my hands, still insistent that I go no further with her. "Look," she said, "your sister-in-law is going back to her people and her gods. Go back with her." I took one long look at Orpah and the city of my birth and said goodbye to them forever. In a moment my decision was made, and with words I will never forget I made my plea to the woman who had become more of a mother to me than anyone I had ever known. I honored my husband and would therefore honor the woman who had given him birth. I would not allow her to die in the desert alone. "Don't urge me to leave you or to turn back from you. Where you go I will go, and where you stay I will stay. Your people will be my people, and your God will be my God. Where you die I will die, and there I will be buried. May the Lord deal with me, however severe it may be, if even death separates you and me." I could not keep the tears from my eyes, and as I gazed into Naomi's I saw light coming into her despair. She closed her eyes against her rising emotion, nodded once, and drew me into her embrace.

Despite the temptation to stay, I went and followed her completely. The death of her son could not sever our bond, and I would not let distance do so either. Even when she was reeling from her own loss of husband and sons, she still had arms to wrap around me when I walked through my own despair. I will never forget the day Kilion brought me to her. She mothered me like my own never would, and because of that I am in her debt. I am ruined for anything false and surface. The gods of wood and stone no longer hold sway over me. I choose to follow her and the God of Israel, and I choose to listen as she directs me this day.

I stop my reverie and brace myself to carry out this plan. I have to admit there is a longing I did not anticipate, a draw to this man that I cannot explain. Stepping on his land I saw the kindness of his heart in the way his servants worked, in the way he treated them as he approached, in the smile he sent my way. I told Naomi I would follow her anywhere, to the grave even. Yet this advice she has given me seems more than out of the ordinary. It seems risky, foolish, and even in opposition to the laws of the God of Israel. But I trust her more than I trust anyone. Even in the midst of her pain and loss she still has love to give to me. So now I endeavor to do the same for her. I will go to this Boaz and make my request of him. And I pray that he will find it in his heart to see our family redeemed.

# PONDER

How is that for dating advice? Go to the bed of that rich guy you met today, lay down at his feet, and when he wakes, tell him to continue to cover you. Um, say what? This is when biblical context is very important, as is the leading and guidance of Holy Spirit. I'm sure as women we have at some point in our lives received crazy or seemingly outdated advice from other women on how to "get a man." Most of the time they mean well and it may have worked for them. But it may not be the tactic that you want to implement into your own life. Especially if the person dishing the advice doesn't necessarily have the best track record when it comes to relationships.

Nonetheless, this is the advice our girl Ruth receives from her mother-in-law. I don't know if you dig as deep as I do, but words paint vivid pictures for me. A whole scenario gets played out in my head from just a simple phrase. Think about it. Ruth was getting relationship advice from her mother-in-law, the mother of her deceased husband. The mother who probably had many memories of her boy with this girl. Wouldn't she want the memories of her son cherished? Wouldn't it be difficult for her to see her son's wife enter into a relationship with someone new? Yet this was not the case for Naomi. You see, this story is as much about Naomi as it is about Ruth. We praise the loyalty and obedience of Ruth, but we cannot forget that her actions were in response to *something*. The reasons for her agreement with Naomi's strong suggestion had to have some point of origination. And that point, that place, that person...was Naomi.

We read in the book of Ruth that both Naomi's husband and two sons died in the land of Moab leaving her and her two daughters-in-law as widows. We can only imagine the grief that was experienced, especially by Naomi, being bereaved of all the men in her life and away from home. Not even a grandchild to continue the lineage of her husband. No relative to truly grieve with besides these young women. But even amidst that depth of darkness there had to be a glimmer of light that shone, a ray of hope that would not be extinguished. As we read on in the story we know that Naomi decides to return home to her people and Orpah decides not to go with her. Yet Ruth stays. The depth of her discernment and choice making was most definitely to her credit, but I want to highlight something interesting here. Ruth says that she wants Naomi's God to be hers too and her people to be hers. Wherever she went she would go. This shows us that there was something more that went beyond the ties of being married into a family. Ruth's loyalty was a response to the God she had seen at work in Naomi's life, even in Naomi's deepest crisis.

Consider this—the God Ruth wanted to be her God, over and above the gods that she had grown up with and that her family worshiped, was the same God who had allowed her husband, father-in-law, and brother-in-law to pass away. Somehow in the midst of Naomi's grief and despair she *still* presented a faith that was secure and real to Ruth. I don't know what that looked like for Naomi and what Ruth got to catch a glimpse of. But we know that somehow it stirred a hunger in her to leave what was comfortable, to leave a home she could have rightly returned to, to follow her mother-in-law on a journey of poverty, barrenness, but then thankfully, new beginnings.

The key here that we cannot forget is that not only did Ruth find a place in the family of the living God, not only did she operate as His daughter, but Naomi, who wanted to be called Mara because of the bitterness in her life, was also a daughter of the Most High. She cultivated a culture of His presence—whether before her bereavement or all throughout it—that placed a craving inside of Ruth for more. I don't know why Orpah chose to go home if she had been presented with the same things as Ruth. But we can all ask ourselves the same things when we choose what is comfortable versus what is true. It's the same longing that caused the wife of Lot to look back in misplaced nostalgia instead of trudging forward with her family in the rescue God had provided. Her decision to look backwards left an absence in her family, especially with her husband, that her daughters decided they would fill. They each in turn slept with their *own* father in order to continue their family line. But that family line lost alignment with the God of Abraham, the true King and Creator. One of those daughters gave birth to a son who would produce a people who would eventually create their own gods to worship. And that nation would be the place Ruth would grow up in.

That is just one example of the extent of regret, the influence of going backward when God has beckoned you to move forward, to come closer. But thank God for the redemption that He weaves all throughout our lives, and this story is no exception. The obvious redemption takes place when Boaz, the distant relative of Naomi, redeems her husband's land and property and also marries Ruth. However, there is another sweet circle that comes around with this story. Ruth, the descendant of Lot and his daughter, has made the choice to follow after the God her people turned away from. In her simple but profound act of loyalty and faith, she chose to be a part of the family of Abraham and ended up in the lineage of the Messiah. She did not know that when we read the genealogical list in Matthew she would be one of five women listed. I doubt she had a sense of how she would be remembered or even if she would be. She just grabbed on to the faithfulness and reality of the God she had seen in Naomi, and because she trusted Him she could trust even the most nonsensical requests her mother-in-law made.

Oh sisters, may we be women who know who we are, where even in the midst of tragedy we present a hope that does not fade. When we are cut, may we bleed Him. When we cry, let our tears be offerings to Him. Even in darkness, there is a light that shines that *is* Him. And like Ruth, may we be faithful and accountable to the truth that we have received and walk in complete trust and abandonment to the will of our sweet Father.

# PRESS IN

1. What was or could have been Ruth's strength?

2. What was or could have been her weakness?

3. What is the biggest thing she needed to grasp during this time of promise?

4. What is the Holy Spirit saying to you about being His through Ruth's story?

# 10

# *Hannah*

>>→

1 Samuel 1–2:11

## PROFILE

His hand. The feel of his small hand in mine. It presses into my palm and imprints a memory into my heart as we walk toward the temple. I've been trying to keep myself from looking at him, afraid to drown in what simmers just below the surface. If I do I won't follow through; I'll turn back and not fulfill my promise. I *so* want to follow through. Even amidst the pressure in my heart, the dam that is on the verge of bursting. I will look at him now and pray that I can make it all the way to our destination. His curly head is just like mine; his eyes are like his father's. They look up at me in complete trust.

My heart skips a beat. Oh, how beautiful he is, such a perfect picture of when two come together. Maybe I should have said yes when my husband offered to come with me the whole way. Maybe his strength would help me make the last few steps. The truth that he didn't dare admit to me was that he wanted to come to feed my lingering doubts, to talk me out of my decision. But he was also occupied transporting the three-year-old bull, the flour, and a skin of wine, all to offer as a sacrifice. And even amidst his doubts I am thankful that he allowed me to carry out what I had promised. I love my husband dearly and I know he loves me, but this is something I cannot go back on. I also didn't want the moment tainted by Peninnah's negativity. I honor my husband, but his marriage to her after me has been one of the hardest things to bear. My husband has never said as much, but I knew it was because of my inability to produce children. And now here I am, finally receiving what I have prayed so hard for. What I have sown in tears for, I will be giving back as an offering, a gift of thankfulness. My mother is angry; she thinks it is a rash, foolish vow. It has been hard to be around her these last few months. I know that inwardly she is heartbroken to give up her first grandchild. It is not my desire to inflict such pain on her or anyone else. The deepest pain is without doubt my own.

As we approach the steps to the temple my emotions rise. I remember the desperation of almost four years ago and how I wanted to die there, die as I poured out my soul before the Lord. But that day I made a decision. I got out of the way and submitted to just being a vessel, if only the Lord would choose me to bring a promise through. I stop at the entrance. When I cross that threshold my boy will no longer belong to me. He will always have my blood coursing through his veins, but this adorable three-year-old will grow into a man totally devoted to the work of the Lord, a man of God. Maybe he can be one God uses to bring peace to this land of turmoil. Maybe we can see deliverance come for our people again. I lift him and hold him close to my chest, taking in the scent of him, breathing him in, capturing more memories to unwrap in the future. I had willed the months and brief years to pass by slowly so that I could savor every moment with my boy. And now the day has come, the day to say goodbye. Although I can truly admit that there is much peace in my decision, the grief is still a weight on my heart, slowing my hands, increasing my hugs and kisses for my boy.

Oh, my boy. I have watched the children of Peninnah hit their various milestones, each developmental moment met with such joy and excitement in our household. I am thankful I got to experience all those with my son. But I won't get to see all the other changes the years will bring. I will have to watch from afar and pray that I can mother him through the hand of God. I prayed for him and now I will offer him back to the God who is even more important than the son He gave me. I will fulfill my vows; I will be a woman of my word. But most of all, I will be a mother who will never forget her firstborn and whose heart is fully surrendered to her Father. I take in one last, huge breath. The scent of dates and dust mingle with the oil I poured over his head the day we began our journey. He giggles as I tickle his full stomach and run my hands through his hair. No razor will touch it. He is to be set apart; he will have a special calling before the Lord. Oh, what wonders to be seen! And what will be his place in the unfolding of our nation? I have to believe that his role will be significant in our future. Even my longing for him to stay mine will not stand in the way of that.

I give him one last squeeze and tuck away in my heart the feel of his arms around my neck. Oh, my sweet boy, how I love you, how I will miss you. I tell the servants at the entrance the nature of my visit, and with wide eyes they leave to do as I request. As the priest makes his way toward me, I finally let the tears flow. I cannot not say much, but as he approaches I know he remembers me. I am beginning to feel weak in my legs and am afraid I will crumple to the floor with my child in my arms. But just at the right moment my husband appears, his task complete and his strength much needed. He places his arms around me and holds me up, giving me the power to speak with his support. "Oh, my lord!" I cry, tears as rivers down my face. "As you live, my lord, I am the woman who was standing here in your presence, praying to the Lord. For this child I prayed, and the Lord has granted me my petition that I made to Him. Therefore, I have lent him to the Lord." I breathe deep and exhale my air, my trust. "As long as he lives, he is lent to the Lord." I smile through my tears and with strength I did not know I still had, I put my child on the ground, place my hand on his back, and walk him toward the aging priest. "In your care, my lord, I place my son, Samuel."

# PONDER

The room was dark, as was the rest of the house. I sat in my glider, crying physically and crying out in my heart. The emotion in me was one I had never experienced and was almost wishing I hadn't. This was the season in my life that I had always hoped for but never fully understood the implications. There was so much change, growth, emotion, and awareness happening at once. And did I mention the hormones? Wow, I was overwhelmed. I was sitting in that dark room in the middle of the night holding my newborn daughter. Enthralled by the beauty of my girl, physically spent by the lack of sleep (my girl could cry in octaves!), and drowning in the crazy insane love that was coursing through me. It was as if my very heart had been taken outside of my body and was now in my arms in the form of a beautiful baby. It was the type of new mom love that made me give hand sanitizer to every person who came in my door. That made me snap at my husband if I didn't agree with something he did. Made me sleep with my girl on my chest for the first four weeks of her life. I couldn't bear her discomfort or pain. I could not stay in the room with her at the doctor's office when she received her immunizations. Because every prick to her, her cries of pain, broke my heart over and over. It was this love that made me begin to understand a speck of the pain of a Father who sent His Son to be sacrificed. If my heart felt such a bond with my daughter, I could not imagine the pain of giving one away.

This is when the story of Hannah came alive to me in such a real and profound way. Here is a woman dealing not only with the pain of not being able to have children but also living with a rival who taunted her and flaunted her blessings in her face. At least for us, for the most part, when there are people who get under our skin or cut us with their insults, we can get away, we can find refuge in the oasis of our homes. But not so for Hannah. She was stuck with Peninnah and her verbal cruelty. She also had to deal with the longing illuminated by the children Peninnah was able to have for her husband. She was loved, oh, she was loved, and her husband expected that love from Hannah in return. In fact, he told her that he should be better to her than ten sons.

This makes me want to laugh because I can just see in my mind the puppy dog expression on the face of her husband as he tried to make his wife feel better, but unfortunately his words were not enough to soothe the craving of her heart. Hannah wanted children, children who would be the fruit of the marriage between her and her husband. We also cannot even comprehend the pressure of that era, when a woman's significance was determined by her family, her husband, and then her children. Even in the palace, during later eras, the real voice that women had was when their son was the heir to the throne and they were able to become the queen mother. It was then that they had actual influence over the kingdom whether good or bad. Because Hannah did not have any children to call her own, she walked under double shame within her family and society at large.

As you look at her story you need to ask yourself—what is it that I want so badly for God to accomplish in my life, for Him to answer? For most of us, we do have one or several longings within our heart. But then we also must ask—are those based on the pressures of my family, friends, or community, or are they actual dreams that God has placed in me that I want to see come to fruition? It's not that our requests are always wrong or that Hannah's was. Of course not! A child is a blessing from the Lord; we are told to be fruitful and multiply, to fill the earth. Hannah's request was good and godly. However, I wonder how long it took for her prayer to become less about her and more about Him, the God of all creation. Maybe the time it took until she cried out with complete brokenness to the Lord.

We must think it unfathomable to ask the Lord so long and hard for something but then give it away right when we get it. It is crazy; it doesn't make sense! But it does when a daughter realizes that the promise *fulfilled* is never more important than the *giver* of the promise. It does make sense within this relationship we have with Christ when we understand that we must seek His heart rather than what's in His hand. And oh, how He does love to bless us. As a father finds joy in playing guessing games with a child, holding a treasure in his hands, waiting for the moment his son or daughter opens it, so does our Father delight in sending us treasures, love letters, P.S. I love yous. But all the riches of the world do not compare to the richness of His presence. All the answered prayers do not do justice to who He is all by himself. It's the similar battle that Eve fought between what is temporary and what is eternal.

Somehow Hannah realized that, yes, she could ask for a son for her to hold and cherish, as I did with my daughters and son when they were born. It is a good thing, a blessed thing, to be a mother. But somewhere along the way she decided that she wanted more. She didn't just want the promise fulfilled in her life, but she wanted God's purposes to be carried out for the nation of Israel. She wanted a heart fully devoted to the Lord and for the Lord to use her desires to accomplish what was in His heart to do. The promise giver trumped the promise, and she decided it was more important for her to be trusted to give birth to a promise than to walk in the promise herself.

Did you hear what I said? I don't want you to lose the last sentence, so I'm going to break it down in a different way. Are you more concerned with walking in and enjoying the promise of God or in being *trusted* for God to get the promise through you? Let me reiterate, the first scenario is not sinful nor is it wrong. God promised the people of Israel a land that He wanted them to enjoy, to live in, to grow in. But we must understand that in order for these things to come to pass, there must be someone who is willing to allow the promise to come through them even if they never get to experience it. Abraham is an example of this. God laid out all these marvelous plans and purposes to him about the future of his people. But he never got to see it fulfilled with his own eyes or in his own lifetime. Mary got to give birth to the Messiah as we will read in later chapters, but she did not get to enjoy her son for long. In fact, she was told a sword would pierce her heart. Even with the crazy mother love she had for Jesus, He did not belong fully to her; He belonged to the purposes of God that were meant for not only the people of Israel but for the world.

By Hannah deciding that she wanted to be trusted to get a promise through, that she would love to give birth to a son only to give him back to the Lord, she positioned herself to give birth to the one who would change the course of history. She allowed God to work through her and use her son to anoint not just one king, but a second king who would establish a royal dynasty that would never fade. Her son would not just be for her family or a way to alleviate the taunting of a rival wife or to ease societal pressure. No, he would change atmospheres. He would walk in intimacy with God. He would listen closely to the voice of Israel's eternal King and move in complete obedience to what God said, despite what anyone else thought. Even if it meant correcting a king, even if it meant anointing a boy who didn't look like a king. She gave birth to Samuel, the last judge of Israel. And as she offered that boy up to the priest to be raised in the temple, she praised God even then, grateful that she got to be a part in seeing

God's plans unfold. She was not a slave to her dreams but rather opened herself up to carry the dream of God to His people.

Let us desire to choose like she did. I want to say that I would give my most prized possessions, my most cherished dreams back to Him. I think I have at times, and at other times I know that I have held on so tightly, afraid that if I give them away they will never come back. But oh, what a place in Him to be trusted to carry a vision and push it through ourselves without any credit, without any fame to our names, without the promise of ever picking it up again, all so that *His* name will be glorified, all so that His *will* be done in the way He wants it to be.

## PRESS IN

1. What was or could have been Hannah's strength?

2. What was or could have been her weakness?

3. What is the biggest thing she needed to grasp during this time of promise?

4. What is the Holy Spirit saying to you about being His through Hannah's story?

# Prayer

>>>

*Lord, I thank You for the stories of these women during a time of promise. These women stepped out boldly to grab a hold of what was promised despite what circumstances may have said otherwise. We go beyond just learning from their choices into looking at our own selves in the mirror. Let the words that You have inspired about them cut into our very souls. May we remove the lies and remember that we belong to You above all else and therefore can be empowered to step into the destiny You have ordained for us. We will not let fear dictate to us, but we will choose to step forward in faith; we repent of anything that doesn't line up with Your heart and Your ways. We want to become more like You; we want to be the daughters You have intended us to be so that we can walk with full confidence in the plans that You have for us. We love You, Jesus; thank You for dying on the cross and rising from death to make true love a reality for us. Amen.*

# PART 3

>>→

# His in the Struggle

*I am His, and at times there is a gripping that leaves
me wounded, set out on lines to dry after a thorough
washing. Hanging in the sun after being undone by
His beautiful, breaking words. I have heard. Heard
the voice of the one who binds the broken-hearted, sets
in place even that which He has crushed, reminding
me that though I treasure them, some things are really
dust and meant to be adjusted. I have heard His
words. And though they sting with painful accuracy
they ring with accurate truth, and to grasp the grip He
has on me I must release what He surfaces, away with
the shackles I've placed on me, sweep away the junk
that He's uncovered, deal with the underside of me.
For that's what He's after and it's all His after all.*

*He has a right to clean his temple; He
knows the best way to love His girl.*

# 11

# Abigail

>>→

1 Samuel 25

## PROFILE

My heart has stopped. Or at least I am paralyzed somehow because I cannot move. Fear has gripped me like a vice and will not let go. I thought I had mastered it. I thought I was used to the onset of it and knew how to respond, but this is entirely different. This is not just about me but everyone and everything that surrounds. I could have taken another blow, I could have withstood another hurtful word, I could have survived his neglect. Because it would have just been me and me alone. The years of my circumstances have taught me that if I just yield for a moment, I can thwart his wrath from spreading; I can ease the pain for everyone else. But this time, in the seeming eternity of this moment I don't know what to do. For my fear does not originate from what just one man can do but from the army outside of our gates.

I place my hand firmly against the wall and ease myself down on my couch. "My lady? Are you alright? May I bring you some water?" The servant who entered my chambers to bring me the distressing news looks at me with great concern. Even in the midst of the catastrophe about to befall us he looks out for my welfare. They all do. I am thankful that even within the tensest days in my household there is still the warmth of those that serve. I swallow and nod. "Yes, just give me some time." This cannot be it. This cannot be how it all ends. Surely I haven't lived through the misery of the past few years to have it all end in one horrific moment. I have to believe the God who has rescued me time and time again will rescue us all now.

I think of my husband. Oh, what a man I was forced to marry. I am doing my best to honor him even in the midst of the trials, but when will it be over? All that has been asked of him is a grateful return of the hospitality and protection that has been shown to our shepherds. Even a simple *no* would have been better than the way my husband responded to that man. When will he operate with wisdom instead of the lust of the flesh? For that matter, when will he see me as a gift instead of some toy to use and discard as he sees fit? When will he see reason?

Reason. It's as if a revelation hits me. I exhale. I hadn't realized I have been holding my breath this whole time. I have reasoned with my husband many times before, brought gifts and my femininity to the table to appease him. Surely I can do this now with determination and purity of heart. I will not focus on the army but on the man who leads it. I will present my case before him and plead for the lives of my people. If the rumors I have heard of him are true, he will listen. He has to. Our lives depend on it.

I do not waste any time. "Quickly, come with me." I stand so abruptly that my servant starts and then snaps back to attention. "We must pack items to present before this group of men. Maybe our gifts can appease the anger that Nabal deserves." I gather my robes, thankful that I dressed in my best today, preparing for the celebration that we were to have with our sheepshearers. My maids and other servants help me assemble a load of items, 200 loaves of bread, two wineskins full of wine, five sheep that have been slaughtered, nearly a bushel of roasted grain, 100 clusters of raisins, and 200 fig cakes. It is a delicious spread fit for none other than a king. We pack them on donkeys, and I send my servants on ahead with the gifts. I need time to collect myself, to breathe, before I follow behind. I stand next to my donkey, one of the men of our household ready to help me up. I send up a quick prayer that my steps will be ordered by Yahweh, that my words will not falter and they will find ready ground in the heart of this leader of men.

Riding toward the area where the men are, I cannot help but marvel at my husband's land. It is truly beautiful and speaks of the great wealth of our family. But the word *family* is not an accurate description of my marriage, unfortunately. There were some memorable times at the beginning of our courtship, when I did not know the full extent of his character. As it was revealed to me I tried to share my concerns with my father. But he apparently cared more about what riches would come his way as a result of our union. I should not have been surprised. One strife-filled home to another. And here I am now, atop a donkey, trying to calm the rage of yet another man, gazing at scenery that should make me feel nostalgic about my home but which only illuminates the distance I feel from this place.

As I make my turn around the bend I suck in a breath. I am not prepared for the scene before me. I cannot even focus on the food that I packed that is quickly being unloaded from the donkeys. The men making their way toward me are not just average; they have the look of warriors about them, a desperate strength and motivation that no army could have stopped. They would have annihilated us quickly; there is no shadow of doubt as I look at them now. And the one who steps out in front of them...I draw in a breath. How can beauty and strength be wrapped so perfectly in a person? He is not as handsome as my husband Nabal or even probably as King Saul I have heard stories of. Yet I cannot deny the presence that exudes from this David, the power, the dignity, currently the anger and maybe, as I draw closer, the humility that I have to somehow uncover. Even as they get close enough for me to hear their murmurs I feel as if God Himself is unwrapping the destiny of this man before me, and I am overwhelmed by the heaviness of the mantle that God has for him.

I slip off my donkey as gracefully as I can and fall to my face before him. I am eye level to his feet and for the briefest moment I do not want to get up. I want to tell him to just take me with him, remove the servants from our home, and give my husband what he deserves. I could leave it all now; I would throw it all away just to be gone from that man. But that isn't what I have come here to do. I lift my head and give a slight smile, hoping I can convey all of my honor and my regret at how David and his men were treated. "I accept all blame in this matter, my lord," I begin. "Please listen to what I have to say. I know Nabal is a wicked and ill-tempered man; please don't pay any attention to him." I shake my head, pleading that he understand what I am trying to say, struggling between honor and truth. "He is a fool, just as his name suggests. But I never even saw the young men you sent." I see that he has relaxed his grip on his sword. He folds his arms, listening, interest alighting his eyes. I rise up a bit more, my inner shaking subsiding bit by bit. "Now, my lord, as surely as the Lord lives and you yourself live, as the Lord has kept you from murdering and taking vengeance into your own hands, let all your enemies and those who try to harm you be as cursed as Nabal is. And here is a present that I, your servant, have brought to you and your young men. Please forgive me if I have offended you in any way. The Lord will surely reward you with a lasting dynasty, for you are fighting the Lord's battles. And you have not done wrong throughout your entire life."

I stay on my knees but lift my head even more, desperate for him to hear me, not just for the sake of my household but for the sake of his future kingdom. "Even when you are chased by those who seek to kill you, your life is safe in the care of the Lord your God, secure in His treasure pouch! But the lives of your enemies will disappear like the stones shot from a sling." He smiles to himself, as if seeing a picture of his own youth, the memory of a giant slayer. "When the Lord has done all He promised and has made you leader of Israel, don't let this be a blemish on your record. Then your conscience won't have to bear the staggering burden of needless bloodshed and vengeance." I sigh; I have given everything that I could. But I feel one more release; I have one more plea. I don't know what it really means or what it will look like, but I have to plant the seed for whatever the Lord chooses to do for my future. "And when the Lord has done these great things for you…" I close my eyes. The sincerity of my next words almost too much to bear, the thought of his look of rejection almost overwhelming. "When He has done these things, please remember me, your servant!"

I lower my head, waiting for his decision, wondering if I am a fool but confidant that I've done all I could. There is a pause and then of all the things he could have done I do not expect this…he laughs, he laughs! I look back up at him and see him look to heaven, sigh deeply and breathe out air he must have been holding in for a long time. It is a sigh of release. The tension lifts from my shoulders and I manage a smile myself. I know that God has answered my prayer. David, future king of Israel, offers me his hand and helps me to my feet. I know then that we are truly saved. But most importantly I know that my God, my faithful always-present God, has rescued me once again.

# PONDER

The response that we cultivate in the most strenuous of times can be a priceless balm of deliverance to others when we are presented with decisions to make in the face of a crisis. I am a firm believer that Abigail had been sowing seeds of honor and grace throughout her marriage and possibly her life. We don't know how she ended up in a union with Nabal; perhaps he was an amazing man who changed as their marriage went on. Maybe it was an arranged affair for money that she didn't really want but was forced into. Her family may have been deceived by his charm and looks, placing her in a marriage built on deception. Whatever the reason, wise and compassionate Abigail was married to Nabal, a hard and cruel man who obviously did not fully see her value or how to respond to and love his wife.

We can allow many things to be cultivated within us. At times we let circumstances dictate how we should think, feel, and respond. We justify our hurts and our bitterness based on what others are doing to us. And when opportunity comes for us to make a lasting, positive choice, we many times choose what is easiest for us, what comes out of the overflow of our bitterness. This is not the approach our Father would have us take. It seems insane, seems unfair, and it does not justify the intense and at times horrific actions of others against us. But when there is a daughter who is grounded in the love of her Father, there is a well of grace and honor that can be developed even in the hardest of situations. We can choose to forgive and allow that seed to grow life within us, a perspective of seeing clearly and knowing how to act with wisdom.

Abigail is praised as a woman who did just that. And it doesn't make sense because we may look at the situation, at the impending doom of her household, and think, *wow, yes Nabal is getting what he deserves. Abigail should just stand out of the way and let justice be done against him.* But she doesn't do that; instead she makes a move to save her household, to save her people, and of course to save her husband. She is aware of his shortcomings and is not blinded to his nature, but still she won't allow his blood to be spilled and to stain the hands of the future king. *It's amazing those two aspects that she uplifts. Honoring someone who does not deserve honor and protecting the integrity of someone she does not even really know.* If she had allowed David to kill her husband and household, she would have removed honor from her husband, who she was in covenant with at that time, and also allowed for King David's hands to be stained by angry blood.

She saw beyond what was before her eyes. She saw past an easy way out and decided to respond in the ways of her heavenly Father. She did this at major risk to herself. If her husband found out about her actions, she could have been beaten or even killed. It's obvious he was a man of anger and pride, and to have his wife approach the enemy would have been insulting to him. Abigail was placing her life essentially in the hands of a stranger she'd only heard stories about and his group of warriors. She believed so strongly in the character and the anointing of David, but as they didn't know who she was they could have taken her and abused her. Or they could have received her request as foolish and gone about their plans. She counted the cost, took a risk, and stepped forward in boldness to prevent a king from behaving savagely. In his book, *Woman You Are a Kingmaker*[3], Bishop Wellington Boone highlights Abigail as one who is a kingmaker. She held honor and respect high in her life and changed the atmosphere with it. Not only did she halt the onslaught of David and his anger, but she also spoke encouragement and life over him reminding him of the promises of God.

Maybe he himself was becoming weary; maybe the trials and the wanderings of his current season were making him more on edge than he had been as a shepherd in the field or as an armor bearer for King Saul. He not only was carrying the knowledge and anointing of the mantle that God had placed on his shoulders, but he was also concerned for the wellbeing of his men and all of their families. Not only that, the current king was chasing him, a king who was demonically influenced and was out for David's blood. To top it off someone he tried to help insulted him. This must have been the last straw. He was done with trying to do what was right and was over being insulted for doing so. He didn't owe Nabal anything and most certainly would not be bullied by him. But then along came Abigail, a balm to a tired soul. Bringing deliverance and encouragement in one moment. Standing in the gap between life and destruction. Laying her life on the line so that the lives of others would be spared.

The decision David made was quick and so was the Lord's justice. I'm not sure if Abigail knew her husband would be judged by the Lord and struck down by His hand. We know that she *did* say to the king that she wanted to be remembered when he came into his kingdom. It could have been a request to be acknowledged, for him to remember the words spoken. Maybe it was a wish to be a part of the kingdom of God in Israel, and therefore a part of his kingdom. Like many other women who find themselves in situations of abuse and neglect, it may have just been a simple cry for help. Whatever the case, surely she didn't imagine that she would be the wife of the king. What a fitting role for a woman who knew how to operate in wisdom.

Within our relationships and friendships we as daughters of the King have the ability to change the atmosphere. Even when those around us are on the edge of making decisions that could be detrimental, we can look past their shortcomings. We can uplift them in their weariness and point them to the life they have been promised. When we, even in the darkest of times, choose to choose Him and His ways we will plant seeds of honor and respect and life and encouragement that can change the course of someone's destiny. You don't have to have the gift of prophecy to speak that over someone's life; you are the daughter of the King, your veins course with His blood, you have His characteristics, and you look like Him. You can speak words over people that reflect His heart for them. You can help them see past what the enemy is trying to dictate to them through crisis and difficult circumstance. You can use the power of your own struggle and let the victory that you have in Christ illustrate a beautiful picture of grace and forgiveness.

# PRESS IN

1. What was or could have been Abigail's strength?

2. What was or could have been her weakness?

3. What is the biggest thing she needed to grasp during this time of struggle?

4. What is the Holy Spirit saying to you about being His through Abigail's story?

# 12

# *Bathsheba*

>>→

2 Samuel 11–12:25

## PROFILE

I can't get over the silk that is his cheeks. They are the softest of pillows, warmest of embraces. His eyes flutter closed as he takes one last drink. My finger that had caressed his skin now lifts away the milky drop rolling down his chin. I release his grip on me and settle him against my bosom. I can call the nurse to take him so that I can get a few more moments of rest before the next feeding. But I don't know if I will ever let him out of my sight. He is the most beautiful creature I have ever seen. Life and health coursing through the veins in his chubby body. I hug him close to me, so many emotions coursing through my heart. He is *one* of the most beautiful things I have seen—I should correct myself. I have seen so much in the last year or so. The beauty only made more poignant from the heartache and mistakes I've made.

I breathe in his light fragrance and remember one so familiar yet different. Some days it's as if I still feel the dirt under my nails again, the sound of my wails that seemed so foreign yet came from the depths of me. Brief were the moments I had with that one, the illustration of the consequences of our sin. None of the fault was his, pure as a new arrival could be; yet he had to die for us, for me. If I could go back in time…the pain is duller now, with this precious balm in my arms, but it's there nonetheless and I will never forget. Oh, but what I would forget is *his* face, so faithful, so loyal, and so unrelenting in his diligence and commitment to this kingdom. That husband of mine who remained so true until the end, he must have known, he must have sensed something wasn't right when he was summoned. He, so righteous, and I, no better than a common whore.

Maybe I could have said no, maybe I could have fought. But I was in the presence of the King and I was undone. And now I sit here, two of my loves in the grave while I clutch my redemption. Not worthy to be in the palace, not worthy to be considered a servant, much less a wife. Yet my greatest mistake has led to the greatest gift. And He, Yahweh has called him beloved. If this one is loved, then I must be too. Loved and forgiven, graced to walk out a story of redemption I will not fail to share with him or those that come after. A few drops of salty water hit the silken cheek of my Solomon, *His* Jedidiah. I sit in the presence of the awesome forgiving eternal King and I am undone.

# PONDER

Bathsheba. She must have been beautiful. As we all are who are a part of this race of women so creatively formed by our Father. Her heavenly Father saw her form and what she would grow into before she was even aware that such love existed. Her nakedness was known by Him and her husband only. The only ones who were meant to know and cover. But there came a time when they would not be the only ones to know. She did not realize, as she took her ceremonial cleansing bath, signifying the end of her monthly period, that there was a king who had stayed home from war. A man who was in the wrong place at the wrong time and a young woman who was in the right place at the right time.

King David saw her and craved that beauty for himself. He would only be satisfied with her. Bathsheba. On a rooftop he saw her. Uncovered he found her and desired her more strongly than he desired to please the one true King. He went to a woman whose husband was off fighting a war for him that he should have been fighting in himself. Instead, he took the battle to that open rooftop and did not win. I am not here to cast blame on him over her, but we are fooling ourselves if we think that temptation only comes when we put ourselves in the situations that warrant bad consequences or outcomes. Sometimes we are just being faithful and diligent in our walk when we are blindsided with an opportunity to give in to our flesh as opposed to being led by the Spirit.

As I watch the news and hear about increasing violence in different places around the world, I sometimes here some bystander or even a news announcer say about a victim, "He was in the wrong place at the wrong time." This was the case of a boy who was carelessly shot as he walked home from school. He did not choose to live in the neighborhood he did; he did not consider the walk he made daily to and from school would be his final resting place. It was just part of his routine. One woman said this and I agree wholeheartedly: "He was not in the wrong place at the wrong time. He was doing exactly what he was supposed to be doing—he was walking home from school." Bathsheba was where she was supposed to be, following the customs of her people. She was doing the ceremonial cleansing that she probably did every month after her monthly cycle. I can't delve into the placement of her roof and why she was so visible to the king. Whatever the reason, I doubt she even considered anyone, much less the king, being able to see her. Especially if the king was supposed to be at war, fighting in the same place her husband was. She may have even been bathing in an interior room that was visible by someone walking along a neighboring roof. Whatever the case, she was there and she was seen and she was wanted.

The king desired to have her to himself and took action to make it so. It was the situation that I would imagine most women in that day and age would have wanted to find themselves in. We discussed earlier about Abigail and her wise move with King David. Even in her wisdom and right choice she still planted a seed, requesting to be remembered by the king, however that turned out. Kings and nobles I'm sure jockeyed to have their daughters be a part of King David's harem. It was a move that would strengthen the security of their land, of their personal kingdoms. Or maybe the daughters themselves initiated requests to be a part of his court when they heard of the handsome, worshiping king. And then there is Bathsheba, the wife of one of David's mighty men, the daughter of another one of his capable warriors, and the granddaughter of his most trusted advisor. We don't know the history of their relationship. It could be that they knew each other beforehand, and maybe there had been something stirring for a long time.

We can speculate over and over again as to why it all happened. All we know for sure, however, is that it did. And that one night of desire led to a snowball of additional choices and consequences. By the time Bathsheba sat in her room with her second son by King David she had lost her husband, moved into the palace, seen the rejection of her grandfather, and held a dying infant in her arms. All from one fateful night of bathing, being watched from a rooftop. I can see her replaying that moment over and over again. Possibly wishing she had been somewhere else then to prevent the snowball effect that it became but so cherishing the infant Solomon she held against her breast. So much had taken place for her to get to that point, and there must have been such a struggle to enjoy the moments she had and not drown in the regret of all that had happened.

How many times in our lives do we make mistakes and dwell so long in what has transpired that we can't enjoy the present restoration and blessings that God has given us? Maybe this is the root of our shame when we find ourselves tripped up by something we didn't expect. We feel like we should have known better; we get frustrated with the progress we are making that ends up being thrown away because of our poor decisions. This is by no means justification for the sin she had a part in. Even if she was completely taken advantage of by King David, there were still consequences she had to bear. In those moments, we can heap so much blame upon ourselves and burden our own shoulders with the responsibility to fix and make right. And she could do none of it. She had no control over what happened to her husband and could not bring him back from the grave. When she gave birth to the son who confirmed her relationship with King David, she had no control over God taking him away after only a few days. All she could do was sit and repent and grieve over what had happened.

Even though the consequences were meant for her and David to suffer, it didn't end with them. The burden passed to a husband, a faithful soldier who was sacrificed for the trespass. It spread to a baby boy, conceived in adultery but still known by God. Treasured by God. He too suffered from the trespass. When we read this it seems so unfair, so unjust. How could someone else pay the price for another person's sin? And yes, it isn't fair. But even in this story of mistakes and consequences we begin to see a beautiful picture of God's plan for humanity enfold. We see a foreshadowing of what He would do through someone in David's own line to pay for the sins of all who ever lived. It was unfair. It was unjust. Yet a Son died on a cross as a result of the sin we all took part in. And the Bible says in the book of Hebrews that there was joy set before Him, and amazingly that joy was us (see Heb. 12:1–3). It was the reconciliation of humanity back to its Creator. Allowing a way for us to be brother and sisters, co-heirs with Christ. At the end of it He wasn't bitter, He didn't hold it over us but said "It is finished" and invited us to come close and be beloved of His Father.

We see this play out in the life of Bathsheba. After all she had lost, she sat holding her son. A son the Lord had blessed her with who was named Solomon but the Lord also said to name *Jedidiah*, which means "beloved of the Lord." After her repentance there was forgiveness and a restoration that Bathsheba could never imagine. Out of her son would come the everlasting and future Son who would die for her sin and for all others. But for her in her present, God kissed her with a very special gift. Not only was she forgiven but the son she had just given birth to was beloved. So if he was loved, surely she had to be too. Even in my mind's eye I can see it— the smile of the Father, the welcome in His arms. The comfort and restoration that only He can bring. Your last mistake doesn't have to finish you; it doesn't have to define you. But if you respond with a heart of repentance it can be the fuel that propels you into the arms of the Father and His restorative embrace. You are beloved by Him if you will just let yourself be.

# PRESS IN

1. What was or could have been Bathsheba's strength?

2. What was or could have been her weakness?

3. What is the biggest thing she needed to grasp during this time of struggle?

4. What is the Holy Spirit saying to you about being His through Bathsheba's story?

# 13

# Tamar

>>→

2 SAMUEL 13:1–22

## PROFILE

I try not let worry shadow my face as I approach the chambers. The ingredients and materials needed for my task are carefully tucked into a large basket. I tried to think of everything I would need to create the perfect foods, a comforting meal to bring encouragement and relief. A servant stands at the door ready to receive me. Next to him is my cousin Jonadab. My curiosity in response to this odd request dissipates when I see the look of urgency in his face. Amnon must be very ill for even the overly confident Jonadab to be concerned. I didn't think I could cook any better than the other women in the palace kitchens, and I'm not sure why I would be summoned over his mother. I assume that maybe my presence will help alleviate the pallor of sickness. Amnon always tells me that I make him laugh like none of our other siblings do. He is always teasing me in his charming way. Hopefully I can bring some joy now.

"How is he?" I whisper when I get closer to the door. Jonadab smiles slightly, a strange light in his eyes. "Better, now that you are here." He brushes past the servant and opens the door for me himself, leading the way. I breathe a sigh of relief to see other servants there, bustling about to make Amnon as comfortable as possible. It would not do well for the kingdom to have the oldest son of David sick and gone before his time. I also can't help feeling relieved to know that I will not be alone as I prepare the meal in his chambers. I assured my mother repeatedly that there would be plenty of chaperones, as I myself had been assured. It is not fitting for a young woman like me to be in the chambers of a man, even if he is my half-brother. Even if he is ill and confined to his bed. I glance briefly toward the area where he lies and head over to the place where I will prepare the meal. It is close enough for him to smell the scent of the food without disturbing him with my noise. Close enough for him to watch me...

>>→

I don't know if it is moments or days later. Ash filled fingernails clutch tightly to rags. For rags is what they are now. They had torn so easily, like the parchment that held my father's songs. Once the symbol of my glory and position, now just a reminder of how far I've fallen. Falling was not my intention; I was pushed over the edge. Placed in a position that I never asked for, now I have to live with not just the consequences of someone's choice...but the emptiness left in its wake. How I can still have strength remaining to even walk is a mystery. I think of all that is drained from me, fought from me, a bitter battle of defeat. Even the cries that propel me forward die on my lips and the pain in my body molds with the excruciating heartbreak on the inside until I cannot tell one from the other, until I am numb from it. I am separated, the rags that used to be riches hanging loosely in my hand, representing all that is lost and that can never be regained again. I sink to my knees at the threshold of my brother's home and cover my head with my hands. It was not sufficient; my cover had been torn from me. I wasn't protected. Nor are my arms enough to stop the tremble making its way throughout my body, coming from my core outward. Disbelief and shock soon make their way into devastation at the full realization of who I now am.

I never imagined this extreme, not even in my worst nightmares. I had gone to serve but instead had been served up to satisfy the appetite of someone else. What will happen to my impending betrothal? Would I ever be able to give birth to children? Who will be there for me in my next moments and my last? How can one person, one moment change so much? The questions pour through my heart and mind until I cover my ears, trying to drown the sound of the voices that come from without and within. I will never be the same again. I am a woman…desolate.

# PONDER

No story in the Bible breaks my heart like that of Tamar, daughter of King David. Not a lot of people talk about her. You probably won't find a five-point message, an in-depth blog, or a meaningful podcast focused on her life as outlined in the Word of God. I guess we look at her and see no happy ending to the story so we leave it at that. Uncomfortable at the scenario, pity for what she had to endure. But that may be the mistake we've made with many women. We look at those who have suffered at the hands of others in pity, but sometimes because of our own discomfort we silence the cry that was intended to propel them to freedom. Or maybe when we look at Tamar it's like looking in a mirror at our own stories, our own suffering, our own silence. So instead of letting out the honest cries that release our pain, we hold it all in.

The story of Tamar in the way the biblical narrative is laid out is right after the situation with David and Bathsheba. This placement is significant to me. I wonder how much this adulterous act affected the daughters of David. Maybe they didn't realize it so much then. But in this story we see a father who is bold enough to uncover his marriage (or in his case, *marriages*) and open the door for another woman to come in. We think about sons watching their fathers, but what about daughters watching their fathers? Who will show them the standard at which they should be treated if fathers do not?

Tamar lived under the covering of not just a mere man but the one whom all of Israel looked up to. King David, slayer of giants, of tens of thousands. Warrior king. Worshiper of God. Poetry and prophetic intertwined in the man who is said to have a heart after God. Could there be a better father? A man who fought for justice and championed the cause of his Creator. A man clothed in dignity and grace who clothed his daughters in beautiful robes of purity and authenticity. For they were virgins, daughters of the king. Handmaidens of God. David carried the bearing of a king yet knew how to love with reckless abandon. He danced before his God. Fought before his God. And yet he stumbled, in a huge way, and the consequences were not just his own.

Thank God that David was repentant of heart and laid this sin before the Lord for restoration. But I wonder if there was restoration for his daughters. A door was opened spiritually that allowed room for lust in the heart of Amnon and then an uncovering of Tamar, Absalom's beloved sister. They were shown that fleshly desire is reason enough to have whichever woman you want despite the consequence or sin. They were shown that maybe a woman is not even secure in her own home with her own husband. And in this situation between siblings, a woman is not even safe with her own brother. I wonder what the outcome would have been if King David, even after the affair, had made the step to recover, to find a way to physically and spiritually close the doors that had been opened to his daughters. It's a sad, sad story, but one that should not end without hope.

If not hers, then your story also does not have to end without hope. We have all walked different paths and have traveled in different shoes. The struggles of the women who read this are as different and unique as our very fingerprints. Yet your past may be similar to what Tamar went through. You may have been in a situation initiated by someone else that left you broken, bruised, derailed, and desolate. It may have caused you to shrink back from all that God called you to be or move forward with your own will and determination as your guide as opposed to the sweet leading of the Spirit of the Lord. But even you, dear sister, even you don't have to let your story end with hopelessness. You were intended for more than what your circumstance has tried to dictate to you. There is a name God has given you that no act of the enemy can stifle.

Tamar's name meant "palm tree," signifying her intended fruitfulness. She was intended to be fruitful! She was intended to reproduce and to birth life. This was the original divine intent for her. This act of Amnon may have seemed to stop her, but it was the shame that really held her back. Tamar's nurturing spirit was taken advantage of as she obeyed her father and went to take care of her brother who pretended to be sick. Amnon, overcome with the desires of his flesh, raped his half-sister and then was overcome with hatred for her. How quickly he changed; how quickly she was changed. And to make matters worse, instead of redeeming her by paying her bride-price (betrothal) to allow her to become his wife according to Mosaic law, he cast her away. The Bible says that she lived as a desolate woman in the house of her brother. The same brother, Absalom, who opened his house to her told her to hold her peace, to keep quiet. So she in turn wallowed in her desolation while he simmered in his hatred toward Amnon. Think about what *desolate* means:

### Desolate

1. Barren or laid waste; devastated; a treeless, desolate landscape

2. Deprived or destitute of inhabitants; deserted; uninhabited

3. Solitary; lonely: a desolate place

4. Having the feeling of being abandoned by friends or by hope; forlorn

5. Dreary; dismal; gloomy: desolate prospects

6. To lay waste; devastate

7. To deprive of inhabitants; depopulate

8. To make disconsolate

9. To forsake or abandon[4]

*"So Tamar remained, a desolate woman, in her brother's house"* (2 Sam. 13:20 NRSV). This is one of the most tragic passages in the Bible. But we need to understand that our God is merciful and so compassionate. He did not leave Tamar without a way out of her pain; she was not beyond redemption. I don't know why the Holy Spirit led the writer of Second Samuel to detail her story in this way, but I do know that there are treasures to uncover that highlight the hope that was available for Tamar and is still available for us. We must understand that not only do we have a Savior in Christ, but because of the price He paid on the cross we have access to the Father. One to whom we can go boldly. One who delights in us but also fights for us. And there is no fight like that of a Daddy who is passionate about His girls, His baby girls. He is fighting mad at the enemy who would dare try to derail His daughters from their identity, from their place of belonging in Him.

You need to understand that the enemy cannot just rape God's daughters and get away with it. Women have been bowing their heads in shame and not recognizing that they were meant to have life and have it more abundantly. Jesus paid the price, our bride-price to redeem us. Tamar was meant to be fruitful, and so are you.

Fruitfulness is His intention for you, not shame. We dream of a relationship that we can give everything to because so is the way of romance, a dance that we learn the steps to along the way. I'm sure like a lot of us Tamar wanted that dance, that chance for true love that cannot be limited to just four letters. That covenant love, *ahavah* love as the Hebrews said. She would give her whole heart to him, whoever he would be— gladly, unabashedly because she was His. And that belonging, since the first sin of disobedience that caused separation, our sweet Father has been intent on restoring.

The hope for Tamar who ended up living "as a desolate woman in the house of her brother" was not restored when Absalom took revenge into his own hands and killed Amnon. I believe that this hope was restored in Isaiah 54:1 where it says that *"more are the children of the desolate woman than of her who has a husband."* I believe just about the whole chapter can apply to her. She no longer had to walk in shame, no longer in disgrace, no longer feel the effects of what was done to her. She could be recovered, a covenant renewed because another King was going to bring restoration.

You see, we get to stand on the other side of the cross and see how our King closed the door to the enemy and brought hope. This King, in the lineage of Tamar's earthly father, came to make her whole again. Make us all whole again. To recover what had been uncovered. To knit together the garments that had been torn, to bring the beauty for those ashes (see Isa. 61:3). That is why Hosea 2:19-20 is such an important passage:

*I will betroth you to me forever; I will betroth you in righteousness and justice, in love and compassion. I will betroth you in faithfulness, and you will acknowledge the Lord.*

Jesus Christ, sent by God the Father, paid that bride-price ultimately with His blood and with all the things laid out in these verses. Not only did Jesus essentially pay our bride-price but He took what the enemy had stolen and said that greater would be the children of the desolate woman than she who has a husband (see Isa. 54:1). He said that now she could call *Him* her husband. I believe that He redeemed what happened to Tamar and in the same way redeems and restores the things that happen to us. We get to go back to the original divine intent because our King Jesus has come to make us whole and cause us to be His.

# PRESS IN

1. What was or could have been Tamar's strength?

2. What was or could have been her weakness?

3. What is the biggest thing she needed to grasp during this time of struggle?

4. What is the Holy Spirit saying to you about being His through Tamar's story?

# 14

# *Huldah*

>>→

2 KINGS 22:14–20

## PROFILE

It is a beautiful day today. I crouch low over the fire, preparing the next meal for my family, but I have paused to take in my surroundings. I am a blessed woman. I hear the sounds of servants and children; I feel the warmth of their love and the strength of my husband who provides faithfully for us. All the while war and rumor surround us; idols and false worship fill the mountaintops. The people sell themselves to gods with no power. All this and still…I squint as I gaze into the glory of what Yahweh has created. The people may not want to see it, but He is still God of this nation. We are meant to be His. The sun still shines even in the darkest of times.

There is a pounding at the front door. It is so loud I hear it in the back where I am. There are a few muffled words and then something familiar. They are calling for me, saying my name as if out of a dream. I brush the flour off my hands, the sense of foreboding strong. Time has come to interrupt my norm. I know it as sure as I know every line on the face of my husband, every trait and temperament of my children, every curve of my body. Oh, those curves that have fallen farther south than they used to be. I almost laugh as I make my way to the front but shed my doubts as a rise of revelation makes its way to the forefront of my mind. I know now that what those at the door are to receive is more important that what I knead, more important than even who I am—wife, mother—for my place as a daughter has been elevated. The words I've heard whispered in my ears reverberate through my very being and I know why they have come. Sent by the one whose questions need to be answered.

I laugh to myself now, seeing my hands—worn, dusty and hard. Hands that have delivered and held babies, have made food for hungry mouths, have worked the fields, organized household affairs. A woman in her place, sometimes in shadows, sometimes in kitchens, sometimes forgotten but never by Him. Oh, the God of Israel sees me and it's His words I crave, His words that feed me so that I can feed others. I will feed a nation this day. For that is simply what I am. Prophetess some call me, but I am simply a mother, a wife, a friend, giving of what has been given to me. And this day I will prophesy to those sent by the king.

# PONDER

Why must we always choose? We as humans, as people seem to enjoy putting each other into factions. Forming boxes of our own making to place over the potential of ourselves and others. We seem to be afraid of discomfort, hesitant to step out beyond what is normal for us. So we justify our reticence with an acceptance of our current state. Are we so afraid of what we can become? There are gentle warriors and courageous worshipers all throughout scripture. God is into breaking boxes and allowing His declarations to be found in the most unlikely of places. We would never think of being summoned by a king in the middle of our cooking...so to speak.

Can you imagine the scenario? Josiah the king has just been given the words of the law, which were found in the temple, by his secretary. He cried out as a teenager to know God more, and his prayer is being answered years later in a myriad of ways. His clothes are torn and he is in mourning, for the words that he reads are overwhelming. Israel is in opposition to God. They are on the wrong track. To dig further, to know more, to get clarity, he tells his servants to find someone to inquire of the Lord for him. There were many prophets alive in his day including, I believe, Jeremiah. Yet the servants choose a strange vessel. They seek out Huldah, a prophetess who was the wife of the garment keeper.

We don't know the exact circumstances of her life or how many times she had actually given words and prophecies. But she must have been trustworthy; she must have been faithful to her role as a daughter, positioning herself to hear the words of her Father. I wonder how long she waited, prayed, and remained faithful to the tasks that she'd been given. Maybe she spent a lot of time encouraging other wives, her children, her neighbors. Speaking words of empowerment to herself as she cleaned. Stirring in some pots while she stirred up some dreams. And all of a sudden the king is asking for a word. All her life culminates to this moment, to lay aside all agenda and speak a word to the King. The Bible doesn't even say that she told the men to wait while she took some time to inquire of the Lord. She would have been most justified and admired for doing so. That is the correct thing to do, right? However, she did not take the time to go and hear from the Lord because she had already heard from Him. Her role as a wife and most likely mother did not deter her from being filled with wisdom, knowledge, and insight. *She had positioned herself to hear and now she would be prepared to speak.*

This, unfortunately, is not always the case for us. Instead of cultivating the call of God within our current states, we allow the very seasons we find ourselves in to be the boxes that hold us in. Excuses are made to justify our lack of pursuit based on whatever reason seems the most convenient. We settle for the common and diffuse the extraordinary impacts that could be made on the most insignificant of moments. It's not about looking beyond our situation but allowing God to teach us in those moments. Allowing His presence to arrest us within the mundane. It is in those times we plant seeds for the future, sowing into the purposes and plans of God over our lives.

We don't know how Huldah prepared herself, but she was used to speak words of truth in times of darkness, sin, and confusion. She was called to be an answer to prayer, and her status did not determine her ability to be that. Within her role as a mother, as a wife of the garment keeper, she took advantage of opportunities to hear and therefore had the authority to speak. She had the ability to reap a harvest of insight because of her faithfulness to sow in seeking. We must understand that words that shape kingdoms don't just come from shallow living; they are the result of deep, secret encounters with the living God. It makes sense when we read Galatians 6:9, which says, *"Let us not become weary in doing good, for at the proper time we will reap a harvest if we do not give up."* Weariness comes when we feel as if what we do has no significance or result. It comes when you are praying for a loved one and you don't see the healing you have been asking for. Weariness can come when God has placed a dream in your heart and you haven't quite seen the fulfillment of it. Weariness will come when you lose sight of the purpose and get caught up in what you perceive is being withheld from you. It comes when we forget we serve the God who will not let His words fall to the ground and who will search you out when the time is right for you to declare what is inside of you. At the proper time... Huldah's proper time was in response to a king crying out for more of God. A king who, when confronted with the written Word of the Lord, needed someone trustworthy to bring revelation. He needed a mother who had positioned herself as a daughter and knew the ways and words of the Father.

I don't know how young or old Huldah was, but as I picture her in my head with some Holy Spirit inspiration I see a middle aged to older woman, consistent in her role, faithful to her season. Not being hindered but hidden in Him, allowing her being to be saturated with His very presence. And when the moment came she was ready to speak. She was the vessel He chose, she was the light in darkness...she was an answer. However, the answer wasn't necessarily one that was easy to give. The Lord was bringing judgment on the nation and now she would be the one to deliver that bad news. Do you see the slight dilemma? The king was calling upon her, and this may have been her only moment to speak a word that was on a national scale. She could have held back in fear or even altered her message. But she knew that she had not been gifted to tickle the ears of the king and appease the populace. She was trusted to speak boldly and truthfully no matter the outcome. Her loyalty was not just to King Josiah but to the God of Israel, the Lord of heaven and earth. They were *His* words that she was to be a faithful steward of; they were *His* words that she was positioned to speak in the right moment.

Many times we are waiting for the next season for us to see a harvest, for us to be used. Maybe we are single and see marriage as the promotion needed to have the authority to speak. Or maybe we are married with children and think our time has passed or that our time won't be until they are older. Within these circumstances we struggle with our identity and believe the lie that a title determines our ability to be used. Let me tell you that these changes of season are not necessarily promotions in God's sight. *The promotion comes in the positioning. The proclamation comes through the process.* As you are faithful in whatever season you are in and, most importantly, faithful to positioning yourself before the Lord, you may be called to give an answer; you may be called to give a word, to bring encouragement. You just may be the unlikely vessel God wants to use.

# PRESS IN

1. What was or could have been Huldah's strength?

2. What was or could have been her weakness?

3. What is the biggest thing she needed to grasp during this time of struggle?

4. What is the Holy Spirit saying to you about being His through Huldah's story?

# 15

# Esther

>>→

ESTHER 4–5:8

## PROFILE

His look of fear must mirror the anxiety trying to penetrate my heart. I want to comfort him somehow, to give him some reassurance, but even I don't know how this all will end. I did not deny food for days to give in now, to turn back now. "My lady," he whispers for the fifth or fiftieth time I do not know, but he is determined to not let me enter the room we draw near to as much as he knows he has no authority to stop me. I could kiss his forehead if I didn't think that hesitation, that small pause would weaken my resolve and send me back the other direction. He has become my dear friend throughout my time here. And that time might end sooner than I imagined once I cross the threshold I approach.

The fear of the past is nothing compared to what is trying to grip me now. Back then it wasn't my life on the line or the lives of a multitude of others. Then *my* freedom was the only thing at stake;

it was the end of what only I held dear and knew as my norm. One single proclamation changed my life forever. I was swept from my home with a number of my peers and strangers and sent to live in a place I had avoided my whole life. Most of the girls teemed with excitement at the prospect of pampering and prestige. I cringed at what I would be expected to do, of who I was afraid I would become.

The treatments and gifts were immeasurable and pleasurable. I didn't know how much my senses would change—the fragrances I never knew existed, the jewels beyond compare, and the food surpassed anything I had ever been presented. Yet I refrained, I withheld, not ever expecting to be chosen queen. I was just trying to keep a semblance of myself, so I would still be the person I knew God intended me to be. I did not want to become the self-indulged creation that the palace intended. Through my simple choices and requests, I found myself favored beyond belief, elevated to be the candidate with the most potential. Still, I prayed that my spiritual beauty would be valued over and beyond the looks that others praised. And then, after a night that would seal my covenant, to be either a consort or concubine...I was chosen. I was chosen to not live out the rest of my existence in a harem. I shudder to think that that would have most likely been my fate. Instead I would have a different purpose, a greater level of influence by being the queen. The wonder of that day still gives me awe. It still amazes me that not only would this man choose me but that God would. And now I see why, and every pain of loss, every fear, every insecurity, every treatment and process culminates to this moment. This moment to plead for life instead of death, and in doing so I may never return.

I place my hand reassuringly on my friend's arm—the faithful eunuch who always saw past my outer appearance and valued what was inside of me. "Trust me," I say, "I need to do this." I smile slightly even through my trepidation. I am sure of this one thing. "I was born for this." My words are truer than any other statement made in my life. I was destined to do this, to physically intercede for my people. To fight the best way I know how for their lives. Although I am an orphan, I belong to a cousin who has been like a father to me. I belong to a people whose blood flows through my veins; I belong to a God who loves me and knows my name. And I know that even if this day is my last, whatever fate the king decides for the people and me this day, God has not abandoned me.

One last enemy stands before me. As my friend steps back in grief, Fear steps forward. Assaulting my senses with scenarios, determined to derail my hope and paralyze me with doubt. But I smile in confidence at how well I am loved. It is that thought that fills my heart with joy. For there is such pleasure knowing that you are stepping into the role for which you have been born. No enemy can take that from me now. I, Hadassah, daughter of Abihail, called Esther, the star of Susa, am being trusted to fight for my people in a way I never imagined. I had no control over the fate of my parents; I could not stop what took their lives away. But now I have been called to stand in the gap for *all* of my people; I will see redemption come this day. I ignore the fear before me and push open the door with joy. I will stand before the king and make my request. And if I am chosen to perish, I embrace the sacrifice. I shall be poured out like an offering and God will get the glory until the end. Death or life will not change this. I am and will always be His.

# PONDER

We all have our moments and will all have our *moment*—one that magnifies all that we've been through and makes manifest that which we were born to do. That calling, that destiny, that dream, that purpose. The one that may be formed and nurtured by circumstances but that is only given by the Creator of the universe and sealed by the blood of His perfect, spotless Lamb. We see the echoes of His sacrifice throughout history, and that realization brings to reality the word in Revelation 13:8 that He was slain before the foundations of the earth. Esther's decision to go before the king on behalf of her people is one of the many examples of sacrifice that still don't even touch what Jesus did on the cross. But they certainly point to Him.

Esther's journey is one that many girls may envy, at least the beginning stages of it. Who wouldn't want to be pampered with the most modern Persian treatments, soaks, massages, perfume treats, spa days galore? She was in a prestigious group, those chosen to go before the king and compete for the opportunity to be queen of the most powerful kingdom in the world. This is the romantic fuzzy filter that we often see this story through. And yes, we know the steps she would take after becoming queen were hard, but we forget the pressure and fear that had to plague her every moment. She was uprooted from the only life she had ever known; the only family she had left in the world was Mordecai.

Scripture mentions no other relatives and, even more unfortunate, the scripture tells us that she had no parents. We aren't given the details of why, but we can only guess that Hadassah, a.k.a. Esther, was a young woman who had gone through much transition in her young life. Maybe she thought she would remain with her cousin Mordecai for a little while longer, marry a nice Jewish man, have children, and settle down with her family. This would be a noble and worthy purpose for any woman during that time period and even now. But God had something different in mind for her— not better or worse, just different.

Instead of allowing bitterness to poison the situation she found herself literally dragged into, she seemed to swallow her fears, as present as they were, and walk out the journey in humility and submission. She remained teachable and with a good attitude even with the possibility of not being chosen. You see, if she had been rejected in this process, it did not mean she would get to go home and continue living the life that she desired. It meant that she would live out the rest of her days in the king's harem. She would be surrounded by countless women whose only hope was if the king remembered a name and called that woman to his chamber. And then maybe, just a small maybe, they would have a child that would help keep the king's interest and strengthen his family's longevity. Other than that, life would continue…mundane, insecure, waiting. There was certainly a large amount of pressure to be chosen, if not for the sake of the kingdom at least for the sake of one's sanity.

But Esther trusted her God and therefore trusted where He placed her. She submitted to the advice of those who knew the king far better than she, and because of this she positioned herself to be trusted by God. For what, you ask? For what she was placed on the earth for. Most of our lives really are journeys and processes, but they lead to significant moments that may define our lives, define the lives of others, determine the story that will be written in history. Esther, our dear sister, helped set the course for her people. Her practice of humility, submission, and favor set the pace for her most influential act. For this time she had been positioned. She could have said no; she could have ignored the call to act. She could have exchanged it for maybe an untouched life in the palace if she continued to disguise her true identity. But she came to the realization that we all must come to. Our lives really are worth so much more in the hands of the Lord. The influence we have in Him can be eternal instead of temporary. We can define history with our actions when they are led by Him and when we are in a place of complete trust and total surrender to Him.

God has given all of His daughters various roles in the home, church, and marketplace. Each one, in our obedience to God, is not better, just different. Some of us may be trusted in ways that thrust us into the spotlight or into places of public leadership. We cannot take these roles lightly or assume that we are above correction and consequence. We also cannot assume that our elevation exempts us from doing the hard things, making the hard choices, or making sacrifices. Like Joseph was positioned to prepare for a time of famine and ultimately save his people from extinction, like Esther was positioned to be the king's consort and go before him to save her people from slaughter, so you, daughter, are being placed at a specific time for a significant moment. To help rescue those who are at risk of being spiritually slaughtered by the enemy. You may even be in a place to bring immediate physical rescue to a person in need.

Do not grow weary in the process or fall asleep on the ride, because you need to be well prepared and equipped to recognize timing. Lest we forget there is a promise coming through the people we are called to reach out to and rescue. Messiah was coming through the people of Israel, and our Jesus wants to come through to a people now as well. You are the instrument that He chooses. Play your part well.

# PRESS IN

1. What was or could have been Esther's strength?

2. What was or could have been her weakness?

3. What is the biggest thing she needed to grasp during this time of struggle?

4. What is the Holy Spirit saying to you about being His through Esther's story?

# Prayer

*Lord, I Thank you for the stories of these women during a time of struggle. These women were faced with situations that tested their purity, their integrity, and the level of their sacrifice. Not all of them got it right, but they made it through victorious and redeemed. We go beyond just learning from their choices into looking at our own selves in the mirror. Let the words that You have inspired about them cut into our very souls. May we remove the lies and remember that we belong to You above all else and therefore can prevail in the darkest of moments. We are not defined by our mistakes if we allow them to be covered in Your blood, so please forgive us; we repent of anything that doesn't line up with Your heart and Your ways. We want to become more like You; we want to be the daughters You have intended us to be so that we can walk with full confidence in the plans that You have for us. We love You, Jesus; thank You for dying on the cross and rising from death to make true love a reality for us. Amen.*

# PART 4

# His in the Freedom

*I need to be free, free from the power of Your words over me and what I fear they could take from me. Because that's the fear, right? The fear that drives this emotional, irrational game of cat and mouse and leaves me in the grip of what You think of me. I'm thinking clearly now…of how Your words leave me bound, ever unintentional on Your part but ever so clever on the part of the enemy of my heart. He sends his darts, his barbs, his spears through others' phrases, phasing me out of what really is into all those past spaces that I've tried so hard to leave, but instead I remain stuck here because the place I need to leave is still inside of me. Me, me, me, it's all about, right? Taking the gaze off You, Lord, and keeping me in the center of my eyes. Keeping me in the center, it makes sense, my blundering nonsense, my dance of fear, this circumstance of me tiptoeing constantly around what I think and do, and the consequence has been that I no longer fear You. Because of me what they say has meant more than what*

*You've spoken. Because of me the fear of man has left me breathless, left me choking on the person the truth of who You've created me to be…Yahweh, Father, Daddy, Abba, break this filter, free me, free me.*

*Free me to run, to dance, to speak; free me to shout this purpose inside of me; there is purpose inside of me and it's screaming out my pores; sick of adorning myself with doubt I am pounding at Your doors with adoration because You hear me, there's no doubt, and what I've been seeking by craving their attention I cast to the side because I am Your creation and You're creating me to be a woman who's a bride in the making. Remove the barbs of fear from me; Lord, I'm Yours for the taking.*

# 16

# Mary

>>→

Luke 1:26–38

## PROFILE

"Greetings, favored woman! The Lord is with you!"

I feel the words within me even as the musical notes fill my ears from behind me. I almost do not want to turn around but an odd expectancy stirs me. This voice is like none other I've ever heard. I turn around and then halt, with eyes wide open, my mouth falling more open than I would have liked. I have never seen anyone like him before. Even as the thoughts form in my mind I begin to sense that I've never felt this way around anyone before. Waves of power seem to emanate from him. His eyes speak of knowledge, his expression, unnatural kindness and joy. My knees feel weaker than I can bear. I lean against the wall and sink down to my stool. What is happening here? Who is this stranger who has called me favored? Me, of no significance or stature.

The man bends down ever so slightly; this gesture, however, does nothing to minimize his height. But it does lessen my apprehension somehow. He continues to speak. What he says I hear at a conscious level, but every word falls on me like droplets of sweet water, sending ripples into every part of my body, changing the atmosphere without and within. His declaration has shifted everything, moving me from what was before to what now will be. His voice falls silent, but the pause is pregnant with much implication. Everything around me stills; the environment around me moves in slow motion as I take in what has just been told to me. It is a lot to take in. What is probably in reality only a few minutes now seems like a lifetime as I go through every possible scenario, every aspect of my life that will now be changed because of this one encounter.

I swallow and blink but the vision is not gone from before my eyes. The words of this strange, beautiful being wrap around me, weaving through the thoughts that fill my heart. He says I am to conceive a child. What will they say about me? I won't be able to hide it. I won't be able to disguise the change that will soon transform my body. How will I tell my parents? Even worse, how will I tell him? That thought is at the forefront of my mind. If only I wasn't already promised. If only the timing had been different.

But as I take in the eyes and smile of the man in front of me all those thoughts slip away and all I hear in my mind and heart are what he said about me. I am highly favored, I am trusted, and He, the God of heaven, is with me. Even if no one else will be, He is. My world begins again and time kicks back into motion. The air is no longer still but flows fresh around me with the sweetest fragrance. The scent of hope. I breathe in deep and simply answer. "I am the Lord's servant; let it be to me as you have said."

# PONDER

I can only speculate as to what Mary was really thinking as she stood in front of the angel Gabriel. What would you think as a teenager who had just been told that she would carry in her young womb the Son of God? We've seen the story presented so many times in plays, carols, cartoons, and songs that sometimes we don't grasp the reality of what was taking place. This teenager who was still a virgin would now become pregnant with not just any person's child, but the actual Son of God, the maker of the entire universe. The one who breathed out the stars of creation would overshadow her and cause her to be pregnant with the hope of not just her nation but of all nations. Prophets and prophecies pointed to the coming of the Messiah, and He would come not on clouds of glory but through womb of a girl named Mary. Simple, probably, to some but thought of exceedingly by the one who really mattered.

God had to matter because she was stepping into an arena that she wasn't quite prepared for. She had to place her trust in the one who called her by name and lean into His ways. She was betrothed to a man who in Jewish culture could call off the engagement immediately. She lived in a society that could have her stoned to death for her perceived adultery. Mary would not be carrying the Son of God in comfort and ease. There was the potential for much cost and much sacrifice to carry out the promise of God that grew within her. Yet with all that risk she still said yes. Whatever God was requiring of her she would do. No wonder Gabriel said that she was highly favored. God knew that within this teenage girl beat a heart of true obedience and an understanding of who she belonged to. "I am the Lord's servant; let it be to me as He has said."

There are those who highly value Mary and even worship her, undoubtedly because of her huge role in the birth of Jesus. Yet even with her choice, the only one who is worthy of worship is Jesus. We can't forget that Mary was just a young woman, a flawed human like you and me. She had her own desires and wishes. I'm sure she had already mapped out what her new life with Joseph would look like. The wedding celebration they would have, where they would live, how many kids. I guarantee you that becoming the mother of the Son of God was not one of her many daydreams. But she still let it be. She didn't even try to fit it all into her own understanding but allowed whatever God wanted to happen, to happen. It wasn't perfection that motivated her to make that decision but complete and total reliance on God.

There are many things that God may ask us to do or give up that we hesitate on, ask questions about, doubt, fear, whatever the response. We may wonder why in the world God would trust us with whatever He's trying to trust us with. But looking at the life of Mary should be a motivation to us that we too can say yes when the situation arises. We can learn from her response and apply her example to our own lives.

You are highly favored. Take confidence in how God feels about you. You are so cherished and treasured by Him. We stand on the side of history that has knowledge of the sacrifice Jesus made for us. A Son sent to be wrapped in baby flesh and then grow up to be a man who would become an offering for the sins of all humanity. The ring that my husband used to so lovingly propose to me as well as the marriage band that sits right under it is very valuable to me. I know that he saved a lot just to purchase it for me, but also it is a sign of a promise. He loved me enough to say that not only was he willing to spend this money on me but was willing to choose me and spend his life with me. A gift was given to us that we did not deserve. A promise, a covenant, and seal of ownership. God showed us our value in an unstoppable way when He sent His Son to this earth. Even though the job of being the mother of Jesus was only given to one girl, you need to realize that God is not done planting His presence in believers across the world. If Mary was highly favored to carry the Son of God, how blessed are we to get to house Him?

The Lord is with you. He loved you enough to want to be Emmanuel, which means God with us. He is with you! They are not just pretty words and a pretty name. It is literal truth embodied, the reality of a walk that is filled with the fullness of the presence of the Lord. We don't have to do this alone. It's not a one-sided relationship that we are a part of. God is asking us to step out but when we do He is in step right there with us and really it's us being in step with Him.

"I am the Lord's servant." With this declaration Mary was acknowledging that she didn't belong to herself but she belonged to the Lord. She was His and would walk in a spirit of humility and submission to His will. Sometimes we don't like to use the word *servant* in comparison to ourselves because in our society we don't want to be told what to do. We don't want to respect the authority that has been placed over us because we assume that will take away some of our "freedom." But Mary willingly placed herself in the hands of God. When you submit your life to Him it is there that you will experience not bondage, but *true* freedom.

"May it be to me as you have said." It was not just the words of Gabriel that Mary agreed to, but it was the message from the Lord that Gabriel spoke. She decided that she would rather live her life according to the plans of God than the plans she could make. And get this—she could have said no. She could have refused. But her faith in God—her awareness of how He felt about her, Him being with her, and that she belonged to Him—catapulted her into a place of total surrender and willingness to say yes. And it wasn't some bad tradeoff. She was going to agree with the words that came from the mouth that spoke creation into existence. The same voice gave promises to the people of Israel and humanity. She was going to be stepping into the very stories that had been passed down from generation to generation. She would be a part of the history that was being declared by the voice of God. Those were the words she said yes to.

He is the God we have to decide if we will say yes to. Will we let go and let it be? Or will we be the ones to one day look back in regret? When you think about Mary, I hope you remember a girl who said yes and then the Savior who came through her. And if there is something God tells you to do that you're not comfortable with or that seems too difficult, I challenge you to say yes and let it be. You are known by Him and highly favored by Him. He believes in you strongly; say yes to Him because He has already said yes to you. Be giving. Be available. Be obedient. Be His.

# PRESS IN

1. What was or could have been Mary's strength?

2. What was or could have been her weakness?

3. What is the biggest thing she needed to grasp during this time of freedom?

4. What is the Holy Spirit saying to you about being His through Mary's story?

# 17

# Samaritan Woman

>>>

JOHN 4:1–41

## PROFILE

Have you ever had someone who knew you? I mean, really knew you? Eyes that see your innermost thoughts, ears that hear what you aren't saying, words that pierce the soul...a voice like soothing waters? I have. And I will never forget how He knew me. That day was like any other. Same work to be done, same burdens to shoulder, people who looked me over. It had not been my intention to wake up next to a man I was not married to. But after five times I was tired of the empty ritual. I guess empty because I was a part of it. Me. This bottomless pit that no river could fill. Supposed covenant had not equated to happily ever after, and giving less of my heart would mean there would be less of it that would be broken in the end. If there was even anything significant left to be given. Whatever did remain I was holding on to. I had to keep some semblance of me, keep it hidden, tucked away where no one would be able to retrieve.

I had my hopes, I had my dreams, I had my imaginings of what it would all look like. But who was I to know that men who didn't see things the same way would thwart my picture. I poured my love out like a drink offering, foolishly thinking that if I gave them my all I would get the same in return. They drank from me deeply and then sucked me dry, apparently unsatisfied with what I had to offer. Painting me as inadequate in order to justify their abandonment, so on to the next I went, worse than a prostitute. Receiving no payment for my favors but instead giving my own heart away. Living my life not for anyone's pleasure, much less my own. Just trying to survive and continue to be as much me as possible. Until that day.

I don't know what my initial thoughts were when I saw Him. He wasn't extraordinary in any way, at least from afar. I had dined and bedded with the most handsome of men. Their looks, however, were no indication of the darkness of their hearts. With this one, although He didn't initially move me, His presence was not alarming. His gaze did not leave me as I lowered my bucket into Jacob's well; I could feel His eyes boring into my back. I was used to it and ignored His perusal. Not only was I not interested but also I did not feel like having a conversation with a Jew, for that is what He was. All I would receive from Him was judgment. But there was so much more He had to give.

"Will you give Me a drink?" His words surprise me. Why does He even want to talk with me? "You are a Jew and I am a Samaritan woman. How can You ask me for a drink?" He smiles at me and like a magnet I step forward, compelled to get a little closer even though culture tells me to step away. It is then that I see His eyes; it is then that I feel the power of His gaze penetrating my heart and clearing a path to the core of me, all that is left. I cannot move. "If you knew the gift of God and who it is that asks you for a drink, you would have asked Him and He would have given you living water."

His words shake me from my stupor. Ask Him for a drink? I do not need anything from Him, and where is this water He speaks of?

He has nothing to draw water out with and therefore nothing to offer me. I scramble to shut the doorway that His intense gaze is creating within me. Pride stands at the door of my heart, and I answer with a smirk. "Sir, You have nothing to draw with and the well is deep. Where can You get this living water?" I am tired of the arrogance of men, especially Jewish ones. I prepare to dismiss Him and move along with my day. "Are You greater than our father Jacob, who gave us the well and drank from it himself, as did also his sons and his livestock?" I want to hit Him at the core like He is hitting me. Remind Him that even though His people turn their noses up at us, we still come from the same family. Maybe if He realizes that He won't ask me silly questions. His smile does not waver, yet earnestness fills His eyes and I feel slightly ashamed for my sarcasm.

He waves His hand toward the water. "Everyone who drinks this water will be thirsty again, but whoever drinks the water I give them will never thirst. Indeed, the water I give them will become in them a spring of water welling up to eternal life." Eternal life? Oh, how I wish I could exchange all my history, the temporary people who walk in and out of my life for what is eternal, for what will last. I remember my childhood; I remember my dreams and hopes. Regret fills me and makes me weak. I look at Him sincerely. "Sir, give me this water so that I won't get thirsty and have to keep coming here to draw water." I am not quite sure if we are talking about actual water or something else entirely. But what joy it would be to have just *something* in my life that lasted.

"Go call your husband and come back." His strange request catches me off guard. I back away from Him, feeling as if I have been hit. The word *husband* is almost a curse to me, so empty of meaning, no value to that word. I puff out my chest, my chin out. "I have no husband," I reply; the words come out almost in a hiss through my gritted teeth. I gather my skirts and my bucket, ready to leave. I am not about to stay here and allow this Jew to play games with my mind and heart. I turn my back to Him. "You are right when you say you have no husband." His words halt me. "The fact is, you have had five husbands, and the man you now have is not your husband. What you just said is quite true." I turn toward Him. *Who is this man?* He just uncovered my life without knowing anything about me. His smile is gone but the same transparent intensity, compassionate earnestness is in His eyes and something else. Something I have never seen before, not even in any of my numerous lovers. Could it be…real love?

My burdens are revealed and I no longer have the strength to fight Him. I sit down heavily, tired of it all. I am done with the striving, done with the longing, done even with the differences that are supposed to separate Him and me. "Sir, I can see that You are a prophet. Our ancestors worshipped on this mountain, but you Jews claim that the place where we must worship is in Jerusalem." He leans in, looking intently at my face, determined that I hear Him fully. "Woman, believe Me, a time is coming when you will neither worship the Father on this mountain or in Jerusalem. You Samaritans worship what you do not know; we worship what we do know, for salvation is from the Jews." He takes my hands in His, looking at my palm, as if He knows every line as if a piece of pottery that He is inspecting. He looks up again. "Yet a time is coming and, by the way, has now come, when the true worshipers will worship the Father in the Spirit and in truth, for they are the kind of worshipers the Father seeks." His words are like honey to my soul. I am taken over by the promise that He speaks of, the intimacy with God, can it be, that they convey. I remove my hands from His and place them on my heart. "I know that the Messiah is coming." Tears fill my eyes, my girlish hopes coming to light. For this is the core of them. Early innocence and desires twisted by the ways of imperfect man. I had wanted nothing more than to be known—if not by God, then by anyone. "When He comes, He will explain everything to us."

He smiles again; oh, it is beautiful and my heart fills up with the waters of His love. "I, the one speaking to you—I am He." I kneel before Him, submitting what is left of me fully to this stranger. And I realize in that moment there is more of me left than I thought. Somehow, in His presence my wounded, broken heart is being made whole. Those words set my heart to flight. I take both of His worn, dirty hands in mine, kiss them, and get up. Water and bucket forgotten, I run back to town, the energy of a young girl filling my bones, joy bubbling with every step. "Why are you running?" I hear someone call out. "Are you all right?" another asks. "What is the matter with you?" a man cries out. I stop at the marketplace, out of breath but with sudden laughter that I didn't know was still in me. One of the women approaches me, shock in her face, as if horns grew out of my head. "What has gotten into you?" She whispers, glancing nervously around. I pant with my exertion but put my arms through hers and pull her back in the direction I ran from. I know her story too, not much different from mine. I look around at the small crowd that has gathered, stirred up by my odd entrance into their midst. I grew up with most of them; even though at times they shunned me or talked about me, I know their stories too. I know their brokenness, their pain, their lost hopes and wishes. I know how much they too long for restoration but don't know how to get there. "Come!" I call out. "Come!" I sing aloud for all of them to hear me, locking eyes with as many as I can. "Come," I say softly, turning now to my friend. "Come and see the man who told me everything I ever did." I look around, tears of joy in my eyes, a smile of hope on my face. "Could this be the Messiah?" Could this be the one we have been waiting for, could this be the everlasting one we can belong to? I am setting my hope on that. And that hope I am certain will not disappoint.

# PONDER

"You've made your bed so now you have to lie in it." Isn't this what we often hear? This may be true to a certain extent. There are consequences to the choices we make, but we were not meant to be buried under them, to confine ourselves to them, to identify with sin. We were meant to take hold of the freedom and forgiveness that was purchased for us, that was offered by a man who was destined to die on a cross to pay the price and give us victory in our choices. To remind us that we were His before we deserved it if only we choose to *be* His back.

So...to make this clear to one woman, He went out of His way to a well and simply asked for a drink of water. A small question that would set the stage for a big change in the life of a woman and her town. I don't know what was going on in her heart the day that Jesus crossed her path. The Bible doesn't even give us her name or how old she was. Yet her interaction with Jesus is one of the most powerful and beautiful pictures of His love for not only mankind, but for women. We do know that she was going about her usual routine, walking from town, drawing water, going back to a man she was not in a covenant relationship with. Wouldn't you like to know what made this women have five husbands? The culture of Samaria during that time might have been a huge influence in how she operated, but we can imagine that each marriage, each relationship, each heartbreak took another piece of her joy, her strength, her heart.

We can see this play out in our lives as well. The things that we want the most are sometimes the things that take the most from us. The people we "love" can do more to harm us than our worse enemy. Yet the temporary fix that they bring is sometimes worth more to us than being free, so we remain in a cycle of unsatisfying relationships just for the ease and comfort of not being alone. For some of us it doesn't play out in relationships but in food, or in hobbies, or in our pursuits. We prioritize our lives around temporary fixes because it's easier than dealing with the truth of our state, the core of our longings. We see the same actions of Adam and Eve in the garden play out over and over again in scenario after scenario. And we wonder in the depths of our hearts why we are not fulfilled, why we still feel empty. Jesus sees this in us, He saw this in her, and He goes out of His way to give us another option.

It may have seemed like the strangest illustration to use water as the focus of their conversation, but Jesus used it to grab her attention and make her aware of her need. He could have crossed her path in any place, but He chose the place that would highlight the intensity of her thirst and the solution that only He could bring. Think about it. She had been in relationship after relationship. There was nothing lasting happening in her life besides the constant dissatisfaction. And this man Jesus tells her that He can offer her something lasting, water that will never run dry. He shows that He really is the only man who will be consistent and remain faithful in her life. What a beautiful contrast to the reality of her existence. He pulls her into a conversation that slowly draws her out of her bondage and into freedom.

I love the banter that Jesus has with this woman because it shows us that He is not afraid of our questions, sarcasm, or doubts as long we direct all those things to Him. He sees beneath the surface of the fronts we try to put up and gently opens up our hearts with His pursuit. He didn't step back from the questions and comments the Samaritan woman threw back at Him; He simply responded in ways that got to the core of what she was longing for. We need to be honest with our Creator and ourselves and allow Him to reveal what the core of us is, what is the eternal purpose that He's placed within us. Ultimately, no matter how it manifests through our destiny, that core is Him. And we will never be satisfied; we will never be whole until we line up with Him.

So even though His conversation started at water, He ended it with worship. He reminded her that worship wasn't about a mountain but about the spirit and truth of who He had created her to be. That even though others had left her, there was a God in heaven who was seeking her out, looking for her true fingerprint of worship. There was someone who would never leave her, someone to whom she could give everything over to who would not throw it back in her face. Jesus saw her truest longing and gave her everything she needed. As soon as He revealed that He was the Messiah, she didn't waste any time but ran back to her community to tell them about the one who knew everything she had ever done. For many of us this would not be a good thing. We don't want our business known by anyone else, much less known about the town. But when you get to the point of desperation, there is such relief in someone knowing everything about you and loving you despite it all. And more powerful than that is when that person has the ability to satisfy every need, to be the solution to what you have been searching for all your life.

This is our reality! We not only have a God who knows exactly where we are and what we've done and loves us the same, but He also has the ability to provide for and meet our every need. He is the true and constant lover of our soul, and when He entered into covenant with us by dying on the cross and coming to life again, He entered us into an eternal relationship with His Father, empowered by the Holy Spirit. Why would we not have a joy that's constant, why would be not be filled with living water that never runs dry? This is what has been paid for us; this is what we've been promised. And like the Samaritan woman, you have access to it and now you have the ability to share with others who are lost in the cycle of the temporary fixes.

There is such a beautiful pattern woven throughout the testimonies in the Bible, and this is one that you should not soon forget. A woman changed becomes a powerful agent of change. A woman who is intimate with Christ becomes a woman of great influence in Christ. If that is true then we must deal with and eradicate the barriers to that intimacy, to that change. Remember you are a promise carrier, a seed bearer. You are meant to produce life. The counterfeits that try to sway us don't hold a candle to the one who calls us His own.

# PRESS IN

1. What was or could have been the Samaritan woman's strength?

2. What was or could have been her weakness?

3. What is the biggest thing she needed to grasp during this time of freedom?

4. What is the Holy Spirit saying to you about being His through the story of the Samaritan woman?

# 18

## Mary Magdalene

>>→

LUKE 8:1–3; 24:1–12

## PROFILE

My voice is hidden. Were I to speak, I don't think I would know the sound of it; I would not recognize it as belonging to me. It is somewhere inside; I have to believe that is true. But difficult to hear amidst the storm raging. I could try to look for it, dig deep, release, but will I drown along the way? Be lost to the chaos and despair that beats at my shore until I am pulled under? Death would have been easier than this, surely—the certainty of finality silencing the chasm inside of me. And maybe it's not too late, maybe it's the solution I need to succumb to. I've walked through so many doors...why not that last final one? For currently I exist as a gaping hole, teetering on the edge of sanity, love falling out of reach daily, peace seeming to be out of my grasp. Small decisions and choices opening the door wider and wider until there was no barrier to the onslaught of torment. Driven away, fighting each day but failing each day for a semblance of hope. It would seem there was no hope to see the light again. And the voices, the voices I thought were my own assaulting me with no ending, pounding me into a slave driven by terror.

Until...until He walked in, like the very sun itself approached me and...they stopped speaking. The wars within calmed and oppression lifted with my sins, as if dispelling the darkness with just one touch. Just one word. As clouds rolled away, He called my name and I could see again, clearer than I had before, no more storm in sight. Seeing the choice of repentance as the door that I would run through this time. Those who had driven me were now driven away into the darkness they attempted to pull me into. Their number perverted the picture of wholeness, but He is true completion. He filled every space, closed every gap with His presence. I see me now, I am cleansed, I am pure, I am His. And oh, there is that voice that they tried to keep silent. There it is shouting and praising and singing aloud, because it can't be silenced when true love is found. True love found me and I am free.

# PONDER

She shares the name of many in the Bible. A name that is synonymous with obedience, trust, sacrifice but also can carry a definition of bitterness. Her name so like others but story so different and so powerful. So at the end of her name we put Magdalene to differentiate her, to set her apart and help us understand her in her own right. Many have speculated about who she was and the meaning of her relationship with Jesus. They've called her a prostitute and a whore. Some have even gone so far as to say that she was intimately involved with Christ, as husband and wife are. Despite our wonderings and some ridiculous speculations, the Bible simply says this about her in Luke 8:2: *"Mary (called Magdalene) from whom seven demons had come out."* We don't know exactly what got her in that situation, but we do know that before she met Jesus she was caught up in extreme darkness. There was bondage in her life that only the Savior could free her from.

Being the daughter of Nigerian parents there are moments that fill me with wonder and laughter at the quirkiness and uniqueness of our culture. I have seen the power and passion of lives surrendered to Christ and heard the amazing stories of God's provision in generations of my family. I also know the prevalence of the supernatural that sometimes gets masked in our American society. The stories my mother would share would leave me in shock and amazement at the demonic things that took place when she was growing up. It's funny that even with what I heard as a child, I still felt drawn to reading and watching things that were not the most uplifting or were downright scary. Even within my young relationship with Christ, I did not realize the seriousness of open doors. And these doors opened up the path to fear in my life. But through the indwelling and the empowerment of the Holy Spirit I began to see the reality of what I was agreeing to and began to cut those things out of my life. I, in a sense, began to close the doors that I had opened, doors that were giving the enemy the permission to enter in with his lies.

My experiences are probably comparable to many others'. We live in a society and really a world that plays with the fire of the supernatural without wisdom and knowledge. There are some who know exactly what they are getting into and seek out the power that it brings. But the most dangerous is when we make choices and are deceived about the consequences. I am not an expert nor have the background to delve deeply or adequately in this area. What I do know is that many of us find ourselves in chains that were not meant for us. We become enslaved to the strongholds that *we* opened the doors to. We thought we were in control, but they have now become the master.

This can happen in many ways but especially when we come into agreement with lies. The lies may result from choices that we make or choices that were made for us. When we choose to look to horoscopes or the occult or other avenues to determine our futures, we are coming into agreement with words that are not of God. When we choose to enter into sin we are coming into agreement with a lifestyle that was never ours to live. We cannot forget that sin is not just what is labeled right or wrong but is truly about life or death, about what separates us from the living God. Anything that separates us from Him in turn *is* wrong and leads to death. He is the source and we can't forget that.

Sometimes the lies come when there are decisions that have been made for us or done to us. In times of trauma and bereavement, we may open doors when we come into agreement with fear, doubt, depression, or anger. These emotions come naturally depending on circumstance, but they were never meant to be our identity. We saw this play out earlier with the daughters of Zelophehad. They lost their father in the desert, as did almost all of Israel. However, instead of dwelling in their loss and letting that set the pace for their future, they made the choice to approach the God of Israel and pursue their inheritance. But what about when true horror happens to us? What about the stories of those who are raped or abused or trafficked? Oh, our Father's heart is so focused on those who experience the worst of humanity. There are situations where there seems to be no way out, no hope for rescue. Even then His sweet Spirit beckons, his Father heart calls, and we must pray that our sisters across the world agree with the hope that resides in Him and not with the lies that pummel them constantly.

Again, I can't speak to the terror of what some women experience. Especially those who are abused constantly, consistently, at the whim of lustful people who are motivated by an enemy whose only desire is to steal, kill, and destroy. This may be what Mary Magdalene experienced. Her situation could have been the result of years of choices made for her and against her leading her to come into agreement with lies and allow them to become her identity. Or maybe she chose to open the door herself in what she aligned herself with, in the lifestyle she chose. Either way a path was cleared for not only fear to rule her life but for it to possess her life. She was engulfed in darkness with no way for her to get out by herself. Until Jesus. Jesus. He was her only hope and her way out, and through Him she was freed from her darkness.

From there Mary called Magdalene never looked back. She immediately followed Jesus and supported Him along with other women. She experienced the teachings of Jesus and His miracles. Every time He cast out a demon in someone else she probably did her own dance of victory and cried more tears, remembering the deliverance that Jesus had brought to her. She personally knew the one who had dominion over darkness. And even in the most seemingly hopeless moment of her life, when the one who had brought so much light to her was hanging painfully on a cross, she stayed. She did not leave the one who had not left her. Think about it—only she, John, and the mother of Christ remained at the cross.

I had a conversation with one of my friends about this, and she summed it up beautifully when she stated that of course Mary stayed. She had seen so much darkness in her life and had been delivered from so much that she didn't run from the horror of the cross. She would not allow fear to dominate her again but decided to be faithful to the end...and the beginning. She didn't allow fear to keep her away from the tomb, and because of her love for the one who loved her first she got to see Him first. She, the former demoniac, the one from whom seven demons had been driven. She, the one who either opened the door to bondage herself or came into agreement with lies when choices were made for her. She who was once blind but could now see. She got to be the first one to preach the gospel, to declare that Jesus had risen. Mary was able to see first-hand that Jesus was who He said He was and that He could surely do what He said He could do!

Sweet sister, do you understand that your potential for purpose can be just like hers? You may not be dealing with actual possession, but maybe there is heavy oppression in your life. Or it can manifest in your fear, the emotions that rule you, or the fruit you produce. Or it can simply determine, as in the story of Eve, what you believe about what God has said to you and about you. There are too many snakes whispering into our ears, and we must make the choice to silence the voices and choose to believe what God has said. We need to choose to hear what He is saying. We are not what the lies of the enemy try to dictate to us; we are daughters of the King who do not have to succumb to darkness, no matter what form it comes to us. And in our freedom we have the ability and the authority to pray for those who may still be battling in darkness. We can help them silence the voices that pummel them into defeat so that they can come into agreement with the purposes and plans that God has for them. We can declare like Mary did that Jesus is alive and active, that He has the authority, and that we are so loved by Him. We all need to know that not only can we be freed and whole, but we can also be His.

# PRESS IN

1. What was or could have been Mary Magdalene's strength?

2. What was or could have been her weakness?

3. What is the biggest thing she needed to grasp during this time of freedom?

4. What is the Holy Spirit saying to you about being His through Mary Magdalene's story?

# 19

# Martha

>>→

LUKE 10:38–42

## PROFILE

The men keep coming in—tired, hungry, and slightly soiled. I am elated and anxious. I'm trying to keep myself under check, but the planner in me is trying not to become too stressed. Whatever will we feed all of them? My house is not as presentable as I would like, and oh dear my stained hands and garments speak more of a servant instead of the lady of this house. Well, if I can call myself that. There is not much status in being the sister.

Looking around me I see excitement buzzing around the ladies in the kitchen. Hearing about the Teacher's arrival several of my neighbors came to assist. He is like a magnet, drawing people to Him, sending shock waves into the community. I don't know why He chose our house to come to. We are not the wealthiest, but neither are we poor. I don't know what we could offer, but we must offer what we can. Although I was caught off guard by this arrival, I will still do my best to put forth a good welcome. Let it not be said that Martha of Bethany lacks hospitality. But even the extra hands around me are not enough. The disciples with Jesus looked ravenous when they walked in the door, and we need to move quickly to feed all of them on time.

I hear laughter coming from the room that they have filled, and it is not the sound of a man. It is familiar, it is carefree—I peek around to look...it is my sister. She has placed herself in the midst of this group, seating herself at the feet of the Teacher. My blood grows warm as indignation sweeps through me. How dare she? How inappropriate! I can't believe she would place herself in the midst of these men. Acting as if she were a little girl or, worse yet, a dog groveling at its master's feet.

I place powdered hands on my worktable, attempting to regain my outward composure so as not to alarm the others. My parents used to say I could never hide my feelings. I look around at the other women helping to prepare the meal, and I feel the heat spreading through my face. This is not right; here we are working feverishly to finish, and there she is languishing in the midst of men! She has no right to be there, and I will make sure they all know. This is not the way I run my household. I was not left here as the eldest for all decorum to leave the house. My parents used to say when my mind was made up I could not keep silent, and I was not about to start now.

"Teacher," I begin as I walk toward the men. "Teacher," I say louder so that they all hear me. Mary looks up with a captivated smile, but as she sees my face the color slowly drains from her face. I feel the slightest trepidation; I don't want to hurt my sister but she needs to be reminded of what her role is. "Won't you tell my sister to help me!" I look from her face to His. His expression alone takes my breath away. Such love, such compassion, and what else—reprimand? "Martha, Martha," He responds. His voice meets my ears but pierces into the farthest places of my heart. His voice so kind and full of authority. The voice of a gentle yet powerful king. I would have imagined King David sounding like him. Or maybe what water would sound like if it spoke. And He only just said my name.

He continues, "You are worried about many things, but only one thing is needed. Mary has made the right choice, and it will not be taken from her." I step back, any fight, any word of defense leaves my lips and I feel shame in turn color my cheeks. I attempted to chastise my sister, but in turn I am the one who received it. As the men's eyes turn slowly away from me I try my best not to let tears escape. But as I look at Him again, oh such love, I feel all shame dissipate. I am loved and I'd forgotten what that felt like. Forgotten to look around and take in the ones around me. As I walk back to the other women I do let a tear fall. It is no longer from embarrassment but the realization that life is more than the work of my hands. And even the important job of food preparation does not hold a candle to the man who honors our home by entering it. Never again will I miss my moment. Temporary things don't compare when Jesus is in the room.

# PONDER

Have you ever wondered what your response would be? I always imagined that I would be the one to stop what I was doing, drop everything, and run to His feet. I thought I was like Mary. And maybe I have been for a season; maybe there were moments when I made the right choice to choose what would never be taken away. I think a lot of us think we are like Mary or at least want to be. We want to be the one who leaves it all behind to sit at the Lord's feet. The one who doesn't care what anyone thinks and interrupts a moment to take advantage of an even greater one. The one who listens, the one who cares, the one so discerning that she can grasp the significance of His presence. I thought I was her. And maybe I have been in certain seasons. But most of the time, if I'm honest with myself, I'm like her sister Martha. The bad-rap Martha who complained and pointed fingers. The one who felt rejected and unnoticed and who was using works to determine her worth. Yikes. I don't mean to be so harsh toward this sister. But in this situation we see a sister who is more concerned with what her sister is *not* doing instead of who she is with. A finger is pointed to shift perspective away from her own lack of desire.

But there is something about getting a tad older, passing through more years on the earth. It allows one to experience more—more love, more heartache, more promises, more disappointments, more freedom, more fear. And instead of seizing moments we size them up, lay them out, inspect and dissect to produce the best possible outcome and image. We succumb to the demands of social expectation and tradition instead of leaning in to grasp the divine whispers that could change our lives forever. This is our dilemma, and I believe it was Martha's too.

We know that Martha *was* doing a good work because her guests needed to eat. It was her responsibility to show hospitality. She was fulfilling a role that was valuable, yet she didn't seem content in this service. Instead of quietly pulling her sister aside she tried to publicly shame Mary to get Jesus to see her perspective. Therefore, her own insecurities were put on display. And I don't want to skim over them. I don't want to dance over Martha's issues because I see how her response points to traits in me. In this story of sisters we see a prime example of the difference between being and doing. The Bible never states that Martha's doing was wrong but that Mary's being was the better choice. I don't want to talk too much about Mary here because she has her own story to share in the next chapter.

So what was Martha's story? What were the circumstances that surrounded her home? We know that she lived with both her sister and brother. This brother, Lazarus, was the one Jesus raised from the dead. The Bible never talks about her parents, so we can assume that they were not alive. So in this situation it seems that Martha took on a very maternal role, yet with the usual frustrations that accompany groups of siblings. Maybe Mary was a space cadet who was always off daydreaming or shirking her chores. Maybe Lazarus never took out the trash or worked long hours and so was too tired to assist. Or maybe Martha had once been betrothed, with a love of her own. Maybe she had been on the cusp of her own happy beginning, of her childhood dreams coming true, only to have them come crashing down with some terrible crisis. We don't know for sure, but it could have been the death of her parents. If so, she had the double burden of dealing with the grief of loss and the weight of responsibility. Of course, the latter scenario comes more from my imagination, but we would be foolish to not delve deeper into this story and pull out the flesh and blood woman Martha was. She wasn't just an example of an overworked tattle-teller. She was a woman who had her share of frustrations and disappointments, who probably had hope deferred and the last thing she needed was for her sister to be groveling all over this Teacher's feet instead of helping her. She is the one we may be like most days—the one who seemed to fail in one instant yet soared in another.

The first time we meet her, Jesus is at her house with His disciples. This scene is laid out for us in Luke 10:38–42. She is preparing food for the guests, an honorable and valid thing to do. But a strange thing was occurring that broke societal norms. Instead of being a part of the food prep, Martha's sister Mary sat at Jesus's feet, listening to everything He was saying. She was not just eavesdropping on the outskirts but boldly and humbly placing herself in the middle of the action to take in everything.

In this moment, Martha had a few options to choose from. She could continue the preparation and ignore her sister. She could quietly pull Mary aside and share her opinion, or she could have moved in closer herself to hear what was so interesting. Instead, she made a choice that so many of us make daily, even the best of us. She used her voice to call out her sister in front of everyone in the room. She used her boldness to approach Jesus and expose her sister's perceived mistake. She used her discernment to determine where she thought her sister's rightful place was. She didn't even dignify her sister by speaking directly to her but instead turned to Jesus and said in so many words, "Don't You care that my sister has left me to do all the work? Tell her to help me!"

Martha made a decision in the midst of her distraction. A similar decision to ones we make in our homes, in our schools, in our jobs, in our ministry, in whatever leadership role the Lord has given us stewardship over. We get so caught up in our roles that our expectations shift from why we are doing what we do to what others should be doing in response to what we do. Many times we get so distracted with the "doing" that we forget the "being." We miss our moments to just be with Jesus. We forget that nothing else matters when Jesus is in the room. When our focus is off of Him we lose perspective on what really matters in our daily interactions and don't use our gifts and talents the way the Holy Spirit intended.

Maybe we think if we operate this way in our businesses or ministries the Lord will justify our insight and take our side in pointing the finger at our sisters, the ones who may not seem to be producing as well. Yet that was not the case in this story and I dare say in our lives either. Jesus replied simply yet powerfully to Martha's request. "Martha, Martha, you are worried and upset about many things, but only one thing is needed. Mary has made the right choice, and it will not be taken from her."

Jesus wasn't necessarily taking Mary's side or saying that she was the better person. Only that she had chosen better and that choice was Him. He is more important than our daily tasks and chores. He's more important than our attempts to impress, more than our strategies and agendas in business. Being with Jesus is the better choice and will never be taken away from us. It is the intimacy with Him that produces influence that will not fade. It's the type of influence that leaves a lingering scent when you walk into a room because you've been with Jesus and His residue continues to reside with you, leaving its mark on those you come in contact with. Our tasks and work are forgettable, but the presence we carry with our works is not. That's what Mary was after, and that is what Jesus wanted to remind Martha of.

Do you see yourself now? Do you see where you can be found in these pages? If you are married and/or a mother, this picture is an obviously familiar one. How many times do you wish your spouse or children would do more to lift your load? You see how much fun the kids have with their dad and wish that you could be the "fun" parent. But you have a household to run, someone has to get food on the table, someone has to take care of what won't take care of itself. Or maybe you are young or single or both. Maybe you don't understand why others around you get away with things you never could. Why is it that you seem to put in all the work but the favor and recognition always rests with your seemingly lackluster coworker? Or why are you the one who always has to wear the bridesmaid dresses while she gets to wear the white dress?

It's not fair! We cry in the depths of our hearts or to the top of our lungs. Resentment skewing our perspective, bitterness clouding our judgment. And in the midst of our perceived mistreatment we might miss our moment. Our moment to just be, to just be His. We were created not to do works but to enjoy the relationship that *His* work bought. Our first calling is reconciliation with our Father and constant communion with Him. We miss our moments for this, and so moments have to be made up. The Bible says that creation groans and waits for the manifestation of the sons of God. We miss our moments to manifest who we are when we get caught up with the doing.

There are times the dishes and chores can wait and you can order a pizza and be with your family. True motherhood doesn't rise out of how well you do household work, but out of your ability to be a mother. The child you carried in your womb, the child you carried in your heart who became the one you got to carry in your arms through adoption. The care of your house should come out of the overflow of who you are as a wife, who you are as a mother. In work and other relationships, there must be a grasp of who you are within those contexts and then let your doings flow from that. Maybe you have been praying and dreaming about a man to enter your life, but when you put your full confidence and contentment in the Lord you can be the friend he has enabled you to be and rejoice with whoever else is rejoicing.

Don't miss your moment to manifest Him; don't miss your moment to spend time with Him. That is what made Mary's decision the better one. She may have already helped Martha before He came. Or maybe she didn't. Either way Mary was able to recognize that there was someone special in the room and she wasn't about to let this opportunity pass her by. *All the things we do cannot compare to when Jesus is in the room.* Because a choice made with Him and for Him is the one that will last, the one with eternal ramifications. Martha received these words and then had to make a choice. Would she throw off the yoke she had placed on herself or would she walk in the freedom of being and therefore "do" out of that space of belonging to Him?

In the mornings my thoughts seem almost wired to start a to-do list of all the things that I forgot to do yesterday and the ones I need to do today. But always the Holy Spirit plants a stop sign in my heart, and I'm given the choice to continue on the highway of all my busyness. Because those things are important, right? My email has to be answered now, even on my day off or evening hours. Because if I don't do it now it won't get done. Or is it also because I want to see what others are up to? What's their status? What is the last picture they posted? But on the other side there is another choice. To take the road less traveled. The little path that could be a bit bumpy might take a longer time but is the most amazing adventure. It leads through valleys and mountains, through wilderness places and quiet streams. I wish I could say this is the one I choose every day. I wish I could say that like Mary I make the right choice consistently. But I'm thankful that there are always detours. Gentle leadings to remind me to slow down and go off the course I've set for a bit. To choose the path that isn't full of doing but the being. It doesn't mean that the doing isn't important, but if I don't know how to first be, my doing will have no eternal impact.

I don't want to miss a moment with my children. That is the truth, especially at this stage when they grow so rapidly, when every milestone is momentous. But my children are not ants on an ant farm either, constantly looked at under the microscope of my watchful eye, never out of my sight. Because if I operate to that extreme as well I will maybe miss the bigger picture of what God wants to do in their lives. So I choose to live in the moments, soak them in, how often or few they are. Take in every bit of my girl as she lays in my arms, thumb in mouth. The cutest, chunkiest infant in the world. I breathe it all in, imprinting this into my heart and mind. In a similar but so much deeper way I want to imprint the presence of Jesus into my heart and mind. I want to know His ways, and when my desire to know Him outweighs my desire to do for Him I will have my priorities right where they need to be.

We don't get the specific breakdown of how Martha responded. But if we fast-forward to another incident in John 11 we may get an idea. Lazarus, the beloved brother of Mary and Martha, has passed away. When Jesus is told of the news and finally makes His way to Bethany there is a surprising twist. This time the one who approaches Him first is not Mary but Martha. I can imagine that this time Martha refused to be distracted and was determined to seize the moment. This time she chose Him.

This time she used her discernment to realize that if Jesus had been there her brother would not have died. This time she used her boldness to speak plainly and truthfully about Him being the Christ, the one who was to come and save the world. This time she used her voice to call out her sister again. But she called her out tenderly, quietly, compassionately from her room. She called her out from her grief and isolation. She called out her sister Mary to bring her to the one who was calling out for her. This is where Martha soared and responded in the way that she was born to. Above all that we find in our paths to do, we are meant to seize our moments with Jesus and call our sisters and brothers out from the darkness. They need to know that someone is calling their name, and that is a choice that will never be taken away.

## PRESS IN

1. What was or could have been Martha's strength?

2. What was or could have been her weakness?

3. What is the biggest thing she needed to grasp during this time of freedom?

4. What is the Holy Spirit saying to you about being His through Martha's story?

# 20

# Mary of Bethany

>>→

John 12:1–8

## PROFILE

I wish the confidence in my heart would steady my shaking hands. I know what I'm supposed to do, but oh, how I wish I could do it with no one else around, no one to see me or ridicule. But I have listened well. I cannot deny Him now just because of what the men will think. I must respond the way I know I'm supposed to, with the best that I have. But oh, if my shaking hands do not halt I may be finished before I reach the door, with broken shards of alabaster at my feet. And what would Martha say of that? Oh, Martha. What will she say of this? My intention is not to bring shame on her or to somehow overshadow how she serves. But knowing her she will not like what I have to bring. I will have to deal with her wrath later. I must move now before my small courage disappears.

I step toward my door and am surprised to see my sister step inside toward me. "Mary, why are you hiding? Won't you come out and see the Teacher?" Before I can utter a word she takes one look at my appearance and seizes my arm. "Why are you dressed like a servant? Where are your better robes? This is a dinner of honor. Go now and change." "But..." I try to get out. "But what, Mary, we are wasting time." "I—" I need to speak quickly, tears are threatening to cross the border; if she sees my tears she will think I've gone mad. But I have, haven't I? Who else would take their dowry worth a full year's wage, what I have remaining of my parents, and pour it out on one man—His feet no less. Who would do such a wasteful thing? But I know the answer even before my thoughts can form it. I would, and a thousand times over. And even such extravagance does not compare, does not put a drop in a pot. I want to pour it out because He is more than worthy of it, I dress like a servant because who am I compared to Him, I give away my dowry because I know...I know He has already paid a price for me. I don't know how He did it or how He will do it, but I know it's done; I know it is finished. And I don't want to miss my moment to respond.

My parents longed for this day, for the awaited Messiah. And I don't know if He is what they pictured, but I know that the prophecies in Isaiah and other places have their answer in Him. I've sat at His feet. I've seen Him raise my dead; I've heard His voice, and I know that somehow I must show my gratitude for it all. I look up at her, not caring any longer about the tears making their way slowly down my face. "I need to do this...for Him." "Do what?" I raise shaky hands to her and for the first time she notices the container of nard I hold in my hands. She gasps and raises a hand to her mouth. I fear her response; she will forbid me, and I will be torn because I do love her so much but I love Him too and I owe Him more. But a miracle is happening before me. She lowers her hand and places it against my face, tears now in her eyes as well. She understands. I see my own heart mirrored in hers. "Yes, sister, you must. It is time for a King to be anointed." And with those simple words she quickly turns around and walks out the door. Before I can contain my thoughts, my sister interrupts the meal and states that she would like to present her sister. She breaks through the last hurdle for me, she opens the door wide. The tears will not be stopped now. I can barely see through them as I make my way to Rabbi, to Jesus, to my King. I kneel near where He reclines at the table.

I do not want to look at His face, but a quick glance shows joy, understanding, pleasure, and sorrow mingled in His eyes. And as if another veil is lifted I see more; I remember the words of the prophets my father would often tell me as I sat at his feet. I know more now and my sorrow and joy match His. I weep as I break that jar. For His body will be broken. I weep as I pick through the shards, not caring about my cuts, for His body will be stripped. I cup that perfume and spread it over His feet, as His blood will be spread over me. As the fragrance fills the room, all the world zeroes in on this moment as I anoint. Everything is quiet, at least to me; I do not hear another person until His voice breaks through, saying, "Leave her alone. The poor you always have with you. She has anointed Me for My burial. What she has done will be told wherever the gospel is preached." I smile through my tears in understanding—yes, that's what this message will be called. And this is how we will respond to it. With everything.

# PONDER

She is my favorite, if I can choose a favorite among the sisters we read about in the Word. I speak of her like this because she understood; somehow she got it. She was aware that there was so much more to the man named Jesus than met the eye. That His very presence signified something deeper and fuller and richer and more redemptive and more eternal than anything she had ever known. Her awareness moved her past being a spectator and into true engagement in every sense of the word. Her act in breaking the alabaster box was more than an act of worship, if that could even be possible. It was a revelation, a response to an invitation that had been proclaimed throughout the history of her country and the ages.

I don't know if she was well-versed in the scriptural text or well-studied in the scrolls, but I can't help but think that she at least sensed the proposal that was being made through the life and ultimate death and resurrection of Jesus. You see, Hosea 2:19 says, "I will betroth you to me forever; I will betroth you in righteousness and justice, in love and compassion."

This was a marriage proposal from a God passionate over His bride. The bride price had already been set and would be paid by His Son. A price the Lord said was paid at the foundation of the world. Mary of Bethany, for that is what we call her, did the only thing that she could think of. And that was responding with her own dowry. Using what she would have given to an earthly marriage to respond to eternal covenant. We must understand that there is an invitation that has been released; there is a proposal that has been spoken throughout the ages, a bride price paid to seal His end of the covenant. We belong to Him, we are His, and it's her story that began to instill this in me. It opened the door of discovery and realization that as women we are daughters of a King and that we all have something to give.

As I penned many of the words in this book, I realized something was happening in the core of me. A flame that I'd been trying to reignite, so to speak, was beginning to grow. Not that I had lost my way or fallen away, but the new season of life that I was in had done a number on my spiritual life. Between marriage, my kids, and new roles in ministry I had to find new and creative ways to spend time with the Lord, and I wasn't always successful. My lack of success led to a lack of drive and then to complacency. Just trying to keep my head above water. I know in seasons of young marriage and young children life moves at a different pace and we are allowed to give ourselves a break every now and then. However, I do a disservice to my family if I am not filled up and pouring out the way I should.

So when I finally took the time to sit and focus, to lock myself in our bedroom for an hour while my husband watched the kids, to ignore the precious knocks at the door and enthusiastic requests from my daughter to open up, I realized I had been missing something. I was missing this—this pen to paper, this fingertips to keyboard. And I realized I had done a disservice to myself by not making time to steward what I had been given. I had been sitting in misery and regret because I hadn't published the many books I had wanted to, but it wasn't about that. It was about simply being who God had called me to be, about taking the gifts He had already given and pouring it out at His feet. The reason for my lack of spiritual fervor wasn't just because of my lack of time with Him, even though that was a significant part of it. But it was also because I didn't trust Him enough to operate in the way He made me, to be true to what He's given me and to be that unique instrument of praise that only I could be. It's not about perfection but about my passionate pursuit. My offering that I pour over His feet. Not based on what others say but a true response to His love that causes the best and worst of us to come out, the embrace of our potential, the release of all our fears, the reason for why we were made. And it is this that is eternal; it is this worship that reverberates throughout history. Not for the glory of men or for fame or social media status. But for the one whom it was all meant for.

I believe that if Mary had not been obedient to pour out her gift, she would have lived in the regret of passing up a moment. And yes, as we've read throughout this book God *is* the restorer of lost and broken moments. He'll take our mistakes, as we read about in the beginning with Eve, and bring about a promise of redemption. But oh, what a gift we would not have the pleasure of hearing about. What a fragrance that would not have been spread, stirring up the best and worst in the disciples, scenting the Savior's feet even as He prepared for Calvary. Jesus said wherever the gospel was preached what she had done would be told. She gave back what had been given to her in the most extravagant way, and because she was faithful in her response her act of worship would have lasting implications. I want to leave that kind of mark, don't you?

That's when it becomes more than what we are doing for ourselves. It's not a selfish act to operate in our God-given gifts when we do it all for him. He knows how to take the seeds of our obedience and produce fruit that is lasting, a legacy that is vital to history. And even if we are never known by the earth we step foot in, we are known and loved by the one whom we belong to. And that is worth it all.

# PRESS IN

1. What was or could have been Mary of Bethany's strength?

2. What was or could have been her weakness?

3. What is the biggest thing she needed to grasp during this time of freedom?

4. What is the Holy Spirit saying to you about being His through Mary of Bethany's story?

# Prayer

>>>

*Lord, I thank You for the stories of these women during their times of freedom. These women discovered freedom from fear, lifestyles, and bondages that were not meant for them. The freedom they experienced caused the atmosphere to shift around them, and we want that in our own lives. We go beyond just learning from their choices into looking at our own selves in the mirror. Let the words that You have inspired about them cut into our very souls. May we remove the lies and remember that we belong to You above all else and therefore carry Your bondage-breaking anointing with us. We are covered by Your blood and repent of anything that doesn't line up with Your heart and Your ways. We want to become more like You; we want to be the daughters You have intended us to be so that we can walk with full confidence in the plans that You have for us. We love You, Jesus; thank You for dying on the cross and rising from death to make true love a reality for us. Thank You for making us Yours. Amen.*

# Close

>>>→

*She is His; she is you.*

*She is not defined by words, words used to hold
her down, cage her vitality and beauty, keep her
from becoming all that is in her DNA to be.*

*From the core, from the core she is His.*

*She moves to a rhythm that is eternal,
cadenced by the beat of one heart.*

*A heartbeat expressed in a myriad of ways,
but the dance is still the same.*

*A move, a twirl and sway toward
that which cannot be moved.*

*She knows where it's all going and
that's where she can run.*

*Distance isn't a factor because there
He is within and beyond.*

*Calling, pressing, leading, guiding,
loving her into the dance.*

*So why should she stop for chances, for what ifs, for the
noise of uncertainty trying to drown out what is true?*

*Those things cannot shine brighter than
the source of light, though they try.*

*The only ones who last are those who reflect the
light. So why should she settle for the lies? She is
His image-bearer designed to reflect that light.*

*She chooses not to be made for them.*

*Twisted and perverted to fit the perspectives of them.*

*Destiny contorted to please the cloud of them,
distortion in the lens just with the sight of them.*

*But she regains all her focus in the sight of
Him, and when she sights Him she sizes up the
competition with a curve of the smile, a sway of
the hip, the flash of her sprint because all else
fades away when she's got her eyes on Him.*

*Simple words do not reign when
He has written her script.*

*And the her that is free is the me I will be. I will be
His. Simply His. Beautiful, His possession of me.*

*Like arms thrown up freely in glad surrender, a
captive of a war that's been waged that He has won.*

***His spoils of war, He spoils me, His girl.***

*It's beautiful, His ownership of me, taking responsibility
for all that He has planned. Shifting me out of
command He takes grasp of this ship and guides me
to rest while He lands. For I am His. Unburdened
by others' opinions of me, He releases the hook that
had me enslaved, tossed to and fro, now He tosses
me as though I'm once again a child laughing in the
wind. I am His. Not anyone else's; He's the highest
bidder; no price will ever outdo the cost of His gift.*

*I am His, and I savor the pleasure
that it is to belong to Him.*

She is beloved. Loved beyond measure and loved into a place of belonging. Circumstance cannot dictate your status; lies should not keep you there. Declarations of freedom have been made over you, a reminder of your place as a child of God. His word is your mirror; we are intended to find Him within the pages and therefore find ourselves. Not to be reminded of how much we do not measure up but to be assured that a price was paid without measure so that you could freely run into the arms of your Creator.

And so here we are at the end of this book, but what I hope stirs up many beginnings in you. He created you. Fit and knit you into a design without equal. The depth of your beauty is not determined by the standards others use but by the high cost of what it took to call you His. His masterpiece, a fingerprint of worship that is unique among the heavens, none is your equal and only one is your Lord. It is to Him we owe our allegiance, the debt had been paid, our shackles cancelled if we choose to receive the gift. Gifted to us is much more than an eternal life of reward, but given to us is a Son, a Spirit, and Father with whom we can have relationship. It is to His heart that we belong.

So do more than long for, find yourself in His presence; make every effort to linger there. Be confident in your place as His baby girl and make bold moves to release shame, reverse blame, break agreement with the accuser, and be known by your true name.

My prayers are for you, dear girl. And if you think of it, pray for me. May we be strong in sisterhood and unity, in holiness and purity. As we have been so sweetly sung over; maybe in turn we can call out words that empower. Let us declare freedom to captives, hope to those who despair. With hands outstretched we can reach for the orphan and widow, reminding them also of where they belong. As we step out in the purpose for which we were created, let us all never forget that we are His and nothing can snatch is from His hand.

# Endnotes

1. Lee, Tosca, *Havah*, (B&H Books, Second Edition 2010)
2. Terkeurst, Lysa, *The Disease to Please*, (Thomas Nelson, 2014)
3. Boone, Wellington, *Woman! You are a Kingmaker* (Provision Publishing, 2005)
4. Dictionary.com

# About Jenny Erlingsson

Jenny serves on the pastoral staff of The Rock Family Worship Center, a dynamic and diverse church in Huntsville, Alabama. She loves to encourage and empower both men and women, young and old, but is especially passionate about seeing the daughters of God be all that they were created to be. Jenny's desire is for the fear of man to be broken off of His church so that they can change the atmosphere around them with their God-given identities and callings. Her greatest privilege is being married to her handsome Icelandic husband, and together they are blessed with raising and wrangling three beautiful and equally fiery children. On any given day you will find her talking loudly, laughing contagiously and loving fiercely, oh and maybe eating a piece of candy or two.